Applied Sprint Training

James Smith 2014

ISBN
978-1-940847-38-2

INTRODUCTION

Movement is the universal commonality shared between all athletes in all sports.

Let it be stated that sport is, first and foremost, a contest of movement. In this way, the actions that constitute the contest of sport are the sum of neurophysiological, neuropsychological, and physical processes. Regarding the physical realm, biomotor, biodynamic, and bioenergetic operations are the executors of movement.

Sport movements are categorized into various finite actions of the joints. While the mosaic of technical movement forms that distinguish one sport from another may be, at first glance, diverse to the naked eye- sport manoeuvres are much more similar and familiar to those who do not allow themselves to be distracted by sport implements or tactics or limit their understanding of movement exclusively to the optical realm.

Intrinsically, regarding processes occurring within the human organism, when one considers the nature of movement, it becomes clear that there are far more commonalities than there are differences shared between the various sport actions. This is rooted in muscle contraction regimes, heart rate intensities, blood lactate concentrations, general bioenergetic likenesses, and more, shared between athletes executing sport manoeuvres in a variety of disciplines.

Extrinsically, regarding what is visually observable, far more commonalities are recognizable between a variety of sport actions when the observer disregards every factor other than the movement of the athletes themselves. In this way, the observer will emulate a human GPS system and subsequently detect the biomechanical linkage of many different sports manoeuvres that reveal the movement likenesses shared between the athletes.

It is through the successful integration of visual/biomechanical and physiological study that allows the coach to maximize their usefulness to the athletes. The deconstruction of any movement based sport problem is thus most effectively undertaken from a multi-dimensional or global perspective.

An advantage is gained when one strives to attain this sort of global problem solving approach. In this way, a freedom to operate is achieved that allows the user to hone in on specific targets at will; and subsequently, return back to an omniscient perspective in order to ensure that synergy perseveres throughout the problem solving process.

Movement as it relates to sport is analogous to mathematics as it relates to physics. Mathematics is recognized as the language of the universe; and any physicist, for example, possesses such a high level proficiency in solving complex mathematical problems that this reinforces the actuality of him or her seeing the commonalities shared between all branches of mathematics.

One sport observation, taken from such a global perspective, is that the ability for an athlete to accelerate their limbs, their body, an implement, or the implement which transports their body, across, or through, the competition surface is a shared requirement irrespective of sport. This holds true regardless if the competition occurs on a mat, track, field/pitch, court, ice, rink, velodrome, snow, sand, or in the water, a ring, or a cage.

More specifically, the ability for an athlete to accelerate themselves, via the land based bipedal sprint action, is often a determining factor closely linked to the sport outcome of a sprinter, jumper, field, or court sport athlete. The act of sprint acceleration is the most potent unifier regarding the specific commonalities shared between athletes competing in those domains.

My professional career in sport began in 2003 and since then I have had the fortune of either coaching or consulting for a multitude of athletes and coaches around the world. My experiences have revealed that deficiencies, and often complete absences, in strategic overall training load management is a global epidemic. The lack of attention directed towards proper sprint mechanics and loading is no exception.

If one accepts that all sports are movement and that sprinting is fundamental to a vast amount of sport actions then one must also accept that its optimization is elemental towards the advancement of sport preparations.

While the bulk of my professional pursuits are, and have historically been, rooted in the development of global think tank strategies directed towards overall training load management, one of the most enjoyable specialist aspects of my coaching experience is sprint consulting and coaching athletes in developing speed and sprint mechanics.

In this regard, I am fortunate to have contributed:

- ideas to a coach of multiple world and Olympic champion Jamaican sprinter Veronica Campbell Brown en route to her Gold Medal performance in the 60m at the 2012 IAAF World Indoor Championships in Istanbul and subsequent 100m Bronze, and 4x100m Silver medals in the London Olympics,
- technical, physical preparatory, and recovery/regeneration support to a group of United Kingdom Athletics Senior National Sprinters and Hurdlers under the direction of British National Team Coach Lloyd Cowan during their pre-Olympic preparations for London,
- consulting strategies for sprinters, jumpers, and hurdlers at the University of Syracuse under the direction of Frank Rizzo and Dave Hegland,
- specific preparations to a variety of national top performers (sprint and jump) at the NFL Pro Day dating back to 2008 and the NFL Scouting Combine in 2010 and 2012.
- training programming for private and distance coaching clients competing in T&F and various speed/power disciplines dating back to 2003
- psychological preparation and global load management consultation to Shot Put athlete Bobby Grace of Youngstown State University who, at the time of writing this project, holds a #8 Division 1 Ranking

In regards to the work of coaches and sport scientists who have influenced my work in the realm of speed development and global training load management, I owe a great many respects to dozens of individuals (most notably Russian, Bulgarian, and German specialists including the late Yuri Verkhoshansky who I had the fortune to work for as an editor of English text). As it relates to the specific content of this project, however, I was influenced by no one more so than the late Charlie Francis.

It is important for me to honour Charlie's name in this manual and shed light on his genius that has unfairly been overlooked by many, over the years, who have naively summed up the accomplishments of his athletes to the use of performance enhancing drugs. Further, in my experience I have become aware of numerous high profile coaches whose programs are heavily influenced by Charlie; yet these coaches fail to credit Charlie in the public domain in favour of playing politically correct charades.

I believe that Charlie was of genius intellect- a true maestro who happened to direct his talents toward coaching.

In many ways Charlie's work has been reflected in my own coaching and consulting roles which span the globe and, as a consultant, my work has reached the highest levels of national and international competition- including T&F, Super Rugby, and an NFC Champion Super Bowl Competitor.

It is essential to credit the late Charlie Francis for stimulating a large portion of the thought process behind the creation of these pages.

This project, representative of my personal and learned experiences over the last decade, will present the deconstruction of theories and methodologies specific to applied sprint training, and its place in the training load, as it relates to enhancing the competition outcomes of any sport that includes sprint efforts.

JAMES SMITH

CONTENTS

I. SPRINT SPEED

As it pertains to the objective measure of speed one must first question the means by which this quality may be evaluated. The most accurate means used in sport are the fully automatic, and expensive, timing systems used in Track and Field; as well as various GPS systems. Alternatively, one the most inexpensive means is a stop watch; however, its inexpensiveness is matched by its inaccuracy due its dependence upon human operation and the associated factor of human error. There are other popular and affordable timing devices that allow for both fully automatic as well as integrated, part human-part automated, means of timing.

The accepted margin for error in hand timing, relative to fully automatic T&F systems, is .24 of a second. Regarding any conversions from from the track to the field or vice a versa we must also account for the reaction times associated with track starts that typically range from .13 to .16. Thus, before anything else, it is likely that the better part of four tenths of a second must be added to any hand recorded time (via a stop watch) for it to be reasonably compared to a time ran by a track sprinter on a fully automatic system. For this reason, the paradigm surrounding the notion of sprint speed in team sports, such as American football in which hand timing with a stopwatch prevails, is, in fact, a paradigm rooted in science fiction.

The means by which speed is measured, the accuracy, is absolutely necessary to provide credibility to preparatory methods. Any, seemingly, hard won efforts gained by an athlete in training whose sprint speed has been monitored exclusively with a hand held stop watch may very well have nothing to do with hard won efforts and everything to do with the poor reaction speed, or generosity, of the person holding the stopwatch.

I.1 ACCELERATION AND MAXIMUM VELOCITY

The zone of acceleration may be defined as the distance over which any athlete is able to accelerate prior to reaching maximum velocity.

Males, on the whole, are able to accelerate over a larger distance than females do to their higher power output abilities. As a result, at the level of international T&F, male sprinters will typically reach maximum velocity in the 60-80m range and females in the 40-60m range of a 100m sprint. Interesting to note, however, is that the bulk of acceleration occurs over a far shorter distance, respectively.

Below you may observe specific results of the biomechanical analysis provided by the IAAF following the 100m world record of 9.58 set by Usain Bolt, as well as the 9.84 ran by Asafa Powell, in the World Championships held in Berlin in August of 2009.

Split Times

	RT	10m	20m	30m	40m	50m	60m	70m	80m	90m	100m
Bolt	.146	1.89	2.88	3.78	4.64	5.47	6.29	7.10	7.92	8.75	9.58
Powell	.134	1.87	2.90	3.82	4.70	5.55	6.39	7.23	8.08	8.94	9.84

Velocities in meters/second

	V10	V20	V30	V40	V50	V60	V70	V80	V90	V100
Bolt	5.29	10.10	11.11	11.63	12.05	12.20	12.35	12.20	12.05	12.05
Powell	5.35	9.71	10.87	11.36	11.76	11.90	11.90	11.76	11.63	11.11

From this data we may observe the following regarding both sprinters:

- Bolt's top speed was 12.35m/s and it was reached at 70m
- Powell's top speed was 11.90m/s and it was reached at 60m

Using those two reference points we may state the following regarding the percentage of maximum velocity that was reached at the various 10m increments leading to the finish line:

Percentage of Maximum Velocity

	10m	20m	30m	40m	50m	60m	70m	80m	90m	100m
Bolt	43%	82%	90%	94%	98%	99%	100%	99%	98%	98%
Powell	45%	82%	91%	95%	99%	100%	100%	99%	98%	93%

From this we see that both sprinters were sprinting at or above 90% of their maximum velocity at the 30 meter mark, 82% of max V at 20m, and 43-45% of max V at 10m. The line tangent to the points of acceleration along the graph is steep leading up to the 30m mark and then the slope lessens substantially between the 30m mark and the point at which the sprinters reach their maximum velocity.

Thus, while the fastest man, and one of the fastest men, in history are able to accelerate out to 60-70m, the vast majority of their acceleration occurs within the first 30meters. While this is not new information, from this, as well as the study of numerous other race analysis, we may deduce that the bulk of acceleration development distances may exist at or less than 30meters.

This proves useful for T&F jumpers, field, and court sport athletes in general as the bulk of the distances covered at the highest speeds, either via the approach runs in the T&F jumps, or on the field, pitch, or court- are well beneath the mark in which most of those athletes would reach their maximum velocity (athletes of particularly large bodymass excepted- who reach max velocity much sooner by comparison).

Strategically speaking, this is where the similarities end. The roles played by acceleration differ depending upon the context. In the team sports, for instance, the faster the change in acceleration (increased rate of speed) the better due to the fact that the ability to accelerate is specific to either separating from or closing in on an opponent or sport implement; which typically includes covering distances well within the 30m range.

Alternatively, for example in the 100m in T&F, the fastest change in acceleration is not always the wisest choice. This is because the finish line exists at the 100m mark and if too much energy is expended early in the race it is possible that maximum velocity will be reached at a shorter distance; thereby, placing greater physiological stress on the sprinter to maintain, as much as possible, their maximum velocity over a greater distance prior to reaching the finish line. For this reason, the fastest 100m times typically result from a race model that includes a fast, yet not forced, smooth acceleration in order to provide for a longer acceleration distance/duration that allows for a higher maximum velocity to be reached closer to the finish line; thereby reducing the lactic period. In other words, the faster and longer the acceleration the higher the top speed which provides for more distance to be covered in a predominantly alactic environment.

The IAAF data reinforces this fact. Bolt reached his 12.35m/s at 70m and, by comparison, Powell reached his 11.90m/s at 60m. Bolt, therefore, had less than 30m remaining to operate under growing physiological challenges while Powell had the better part of 40m.

It must be pointed out that the highest maximum velocity does not always amount to the fastest race time. While this may sound peculiar, we must account for the significance of the start and reaction time. Bolt's 12.35m/s is the highest maximum velocity ever recorded in a 100m competition (some research has him listed at over 12.4m/s at peak velocity). It also accompanied the fastest recorded time in a 100m competition (9.58). Had he stumbled out of the blocks, however, and tripped and fell to the ground he still may have recovered and reached 12.35m/s; however, it would have been much closer to the finish; and while that would have further reduced the lactic period it surely wouldn't have mattered as everyone else would have already long since finished the race.

In regards to what did happen, not only did Bolt register a higher maximum velocity farther into the race, his 60m split bested the 60m world record by a full tenth of a second, and the reduced lactic period allowed him to remain within 2% of his maximum velocity through the tape. The result being the fastest 100m of all time.

The relevance of discussing T&F data, as it pertains to other sports, is for purposes of education and perspective. The fastest Track sprinters are the fastest athletes in the world, regardless of distance.

For example, there have been a variety of track sprinters who have been hand timed (as most American football athletes are) in the 40yd dash (36.576m) at less than 4 seconds.

Those familiar with hand timed 40yd dash times will appreciate the significance of these accomplishments. In this way, there are many transferable lessons to be gleaned from these athletes; and the speeds that they are capable of generating provides a much needed perspective for coaches and athletes in other sports who may have a limited understanding of speed development, the trainability of speed, and it's place in the training.

II. SPEED ZONES

In T&F sprint methodology, not the least of which includes the pioneering efforts of the late Charlie Francis, the following terminology reflects the different facets of speed relative to the distance over which it must be generated:

- Start- 0-10m
- Acceleration- 0-30m
- Maximum Velocity (Alactic Speed)- 50-80m or less than 8sec
- Speed Endurance- 80-150m, 8-15sec
- Special Endurance I- 150-300m, 15-45sec
- Special Endurance II- 300-600m, >45sec

In the sprint training vernacular, intensity is synonymous with velocity. As a result, the highest intensity is associated with maximum velocity and the intensity decreases on either side of it either on the way up or on the way down.

The nature of speed over the zones up to and including special endurance II may be illustrated as a bell curve. Consider the following graph as it appears in Charlie Francis' Vancouver Lecture from 2004:

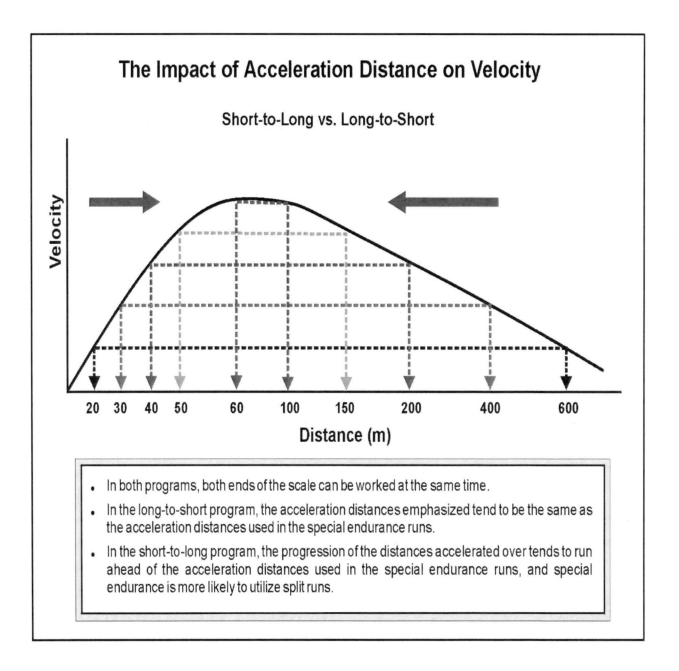

The Impact of Acceleration Distance on Velocity

Short-to-Long vs. Long-to-Short

- In both programs, both ends of the scale can be worked at the same time.
- In the long-to-short program, the acceleration distances emphasized tend to be the same as the acceleration distances used in the special endurance runs.
- In the short-to-long program, the progression of the distances accelerated over tends to run ahead of the acceleration distances used in the special endurance runs, and special endurance is more likely to utilize split runs.

From this we may observe the comparable speeds shared between the distances on either side of the point in which maximum velocity is achieved and how the degree of separation between the two diminishes as the distances near the the point of maximum velocity.

- 20m and 600m
- 30m and 400m
- 40m and 200m
- 50m and 150m
- 60m and 100m

12

Provided the sprinter is moving as fast as possible, the longer the distance over which the sprint is executed the greater the physiological challenge. This is why the 400m event is regarded as, arguably, the most physically gruelling event in T&F. This is rooted in the blood lactate concentrations, and associated hydrogen ion accumulation, generated as a result of the effort. While the maximal velocity of the event is not that of the shorter sprints, the distance/duration over which the work is performed is such that it is both short and long enough for the sprinter to expend a phenomenal effort.

Consider Michael Johnson's 43.18 world record splits (recorded by the Biomechanics team at the 1999 World Championships in Sevilla Spain).

- 100m- 11.10, 200m- 21.22, 300m-31.66, 400m- 43.18
- Splits- 0-100m (11.10s), 100-200m (10.12s), 200-300m (10.44), 300-400m (11.52s)
- His first 200m in 21.22 and second in 21.96

If you have experience in track you will appreciate these numbers. If you do not have track experience you may simply do the math and consider how the bulk of a sprinters maximum velocity is achieved in the first 30meters. While the acceleration in a 400m event is not as aggressive as a 100m event it does not require much imagination to appreciate the challenge of sustaining such a high percentage of the maximum for over 40seconds of continuous work.

III. INTENSITY LIMITS

Intensity limits are an efficient means of setting a governor on the achievable intensity of any cyclic movement.

In T&F these apply to the S-L as the progression to maximum velocity work as well as a means of executing special endurance split runs.

In the S-L we know that the high level sprinters are traveling at or near maximum velocity at the 60meter mark. Intensity limits may be set at any interval leading up to the 60m mark in order to ensure that the neuromuscular demand of the effort is limited to the mark that has been set.

The following intensity limit + maintenance speed work repetitions are common for repeat 60m efforts:

- 10 + 50
- 20 + 40
- 30 + 30
- 40 + 20

In this way, the sprinter is accelerating to either the 10, 20, 30, or 40m mark and then holding/maintaining that speed through the finish void of further acceleration past that point. This ensures that the intensity of the effort is limited to a 10, 20, 30, or 40m sprint which are all degrees of sub-maximal efforts relative to that male sprinters maximum velocity.

The key to the execution of these sprints is that the athlete is capable of negotiating the shift from acceleration to maintenance in a smooth and relaxed fashion. This is largely manipulated by the intensity of the arm action and another reminder that acceleration is a skill.

IV. SPEED DEVELOPMENT STRATEGIES

Charlie's graph also provides important information for both speed development strategies as well as implications on the development of mechanics and revolutionizing the management of overall sport training loads.

Strategically speaking, the long to short and short to long methodological approaches may be taken literally. Either one suggests that the sprinter work from distances that are either longer or shorter than the competition distance; and as the competition period approaches the training distances draw closer and closer to the race or competition sprint distances themselves.

There are pros and cons associated with each approach:

	Long to Short	Short to Long
Cold weather environments/limited indoor training space	Con	Pro
Warm weather year round	Pro	Pro
Limited Therapy Options	Pro	Con
Low Tolerance for CNS Stress	Pro	Con
High Tolerance for CNS Stress	Pro	Pro

IV.1 CLIMATE/ENVIRONMENTAL CONDITIONS

Cold weather environments are not conducive to speed training in general due to the heightened challenge of both warm up as well as maintaining heat in the muscles. As a consequence, the risk of muscular trauma increases substantially the colder the climate in which the sprinter is training.

In such environmental conditions it proves advantageous to have access to indoor facilities. The question then becomes- how big is the facility. The space of the facility determines the distance over which the sprinter may accelerate in an uninterrupted fashion. Maximum velocity work demands a linear path of travel. Thus, an indoor facility that is suitable for the training of top speed must, at the minimum, provide a straight away that is long enough for the sprinter/athlete to achieve maximum velocity as well as have room to safely decelerate. Forced decelerations, while they are intrinsic to the preparation of field and court sports, are also one of the number one causes of hamstring pulls. As a result, there is no need to unnecessarily compound upon the number of these actions.

One option for indoor facilities that are only marginally longer than the distance at which the athlete hits their maximum velocity is to place crash pads against the wall. These are often used in T&F indoor 60m competitions for the same reasons.

In any case, athletes and sprinters who reside in cold weather climates, who also have access to reasonable indoor training facilities, will find that a short to long approach is more advantageous, if not mandatory, as it will keep them out of the weather.

Alternatively, athletes/sprinters who have the good fortune of living and training in warm weather climates have the luxury of choosing either approach. In this case, the questions become: what therapy options the athletes have access to and what is their tolerance for CNS intensive training.

IV.1.1 COLD WEATHER TRAINING STRATEGIES

It is appropriate to discuss various training strategies for athletes restricted to cold weather climates and limited indoor training space.

It has long since been established that supplementary forms of training must substitute for max velocity and speed endurance runs for track athletes who are unable to perform those distances in their given facilities. Even non-track athletes must have ample space to perform, at the very least, acceleration sprints during the colder months. If these athletes are restricted to indoor spaces that are nothing more than weight rooms then alternative stimuli must prevail and take up the neuromuscular slack.

We know the neuromuscular specifics associated with sprinting, particularly maximum velocity sprinting, are unmatched relative to kinematic equivalents. We also know, however, that there are means of generating very high neuromuscular outputs/muscular contraction velocities via means other than bipedal sprinting.

Following are some effective "plan B" strategies that are suitable for these climate/space restricted situations:

Bike

Spin bikes, in particular, offer some unique opportunities to generate both high velocity as well as high force efforts in a cyclic manner involving the legs.

The height of the seat may be adjusted in order to stimulate leg musculature similar to the muscular dynamics of bipedal sprinting. The lower the seat the more the effort is quadricep dominant as the knees never fully extend at the bottom of the pedal stroke. This is more specific to early acceleration dynamics in which the sprinter will make ground contact in a position of knee band far deeper than what he/she will execute in the upright sprint position.

Alternatively, the posterior leg musculature is more effectively engaged as the seat height is raised; which allows the athlete to nearly extend the leg at the bottom of the pedal stroke. In this way, the muscular dynamics begin to draw closer to the upright sprint position.

While the biodynamic structure of bike sprints cannot be drawn parallel to that of bipedal sprinting, the accepted durations for various sprint efforts may effectively be translated to the bike:
- Acceleration: <6sec
- Max Velocity: 6-8sec
- Speed Endurance: 8-15sec
- Special Endurance: I 15-45sec
- Special Endurance: II >45sec

It is essential, however, to adjust the resistance such that the output levels follow a contour that approximates the curve of sprint velocity. In all cases, same as in bipedal sprinting, the volitional effort of the athletes must be such that they are maximizing their output over the duration of the work interval.

Power Speed

Various power speed drills (which are discussed in more detail later in this manual) may be performed with and without overload (holding a weight or medicine ball) in spaces as small as 5-10meters. If they are to be used for the purpose of offering a high intensity neuromuscular stimulus, in place of sprint work, then athletes must adjust their method of execution different from the norm in order to increase muscle contractile velocity. In this way, the volitional effort will be directed towards very rapid movement; though always maintaining fluidity and rhythm.

The following power speed drills are most useful in lieu of sprinting in a restricted indoor space:
- The running A (high knee) exercise
- Modified butt kicks in which the hips flex and knees are lifted as they collapse (as opposed to non/minimal hip flexion with most of the action occurring at the knee)
- Explosive Skips-Skip Bounds

Regardless of what other substitute means are used, in place of sprint work, it is suggested that the modified power speed drill find their way into the training. This is so because it is vital to preserve as much sprint specific movement coordination as possible. While the more rapidly executed power speed drills still do not come near the muscle contraction velocities of maximum velocity sprinting, the overall movement dynamics are a viable substitution in comparison to other non-running alternatives.

Explosive Throws

Explosive throws, with any implement that corresponds to the desired output level, are an excellent means of motor unit involvement that involves explosive hip/knee extension. In this way, the most favourable hip/knee dominant throws are:

Overhead backward (posterior chain dominant)

Between the Legs Forward (anterior chain dominant)

Diving Forward Throw from the squat position (also anterior chain dominant).

These throws may also be combined with explosive jumps for additional stimulation. In this case, the jump, or series of jumps, would precede the throw.

Jumps/Bounds

Various jumps and bounds prove themselves very useful as a means of stimulating the neuromuscular process as it relates to sprinting. Jumps that include deeper knee bends during ground contact are more relevant towards acceleration development.

Box Jump Up + Off into Landing Pit

Box Jump Up + Up + Off into Landing Pit

Consecutive Jumps Up Stairs

Consecutive Jumps Up Hill (Pedro Leal of the Portugal National Sevens Side)

Alternatively, jumps that include minimal knee bend during ground contact are more relevant towards maximal velocity development. In both cases, the impulse associated with the effort corresponds more closely to the dynamics of the associated sprint action.

Hurdle Hops

Any number of bounds (RLRL, RRLL, …) are also highly effective alternatives; however, these exercises require more space, in comparison the jumps already illustrated, as the stride length associated with higher output bounding will quickly outsize smaller indoor training spaces after only a few ground contacts. Thus, these means are more favourably integrated in the preparation of athletes who have access to larger indoor training spaces as well as the opportunity to train outdoors for most of the year.

Weights

Weight training constitutes the last of the high output neuromuscular stimulus alternatives. In order to approximate the motor unit involvement of sprinting it is important to ensure that the weight training exercise is hip dominant and performed explosively. This may include any number of Olympic weightlifting variations, explosive squats, deadlifts, step ups, as well as the use of certain specialized training apparatus that have been developed specifically for sprint development.

It should be obvious that all cold weather/training space restricted training alternatives are, in fact, training elements that would already be included in the the preparation of speed/power athletes. It is here where it becomes important to point out the significance of training repertoire and proportionality.

If an athlete is not already familiar (technical proficient) at a particular training form then it may become challenging to introduce it at a time when no other viable alternative is available. This may be due to either the technical complexity of the exercise (i.e. barbell snatches) or the risk of inducing adaptation stiffness. Thus, building a comprehensive training repertoire proves highly advantageous for athletes.

Load proportionality is the defining characteristic regarding cold weather/limited training space alternatives. Ideally, the athlete will already be proficient in the movements that will serve as the sprint substitute. In this way, the volume of these "plan B" substitutes will increase substantially in lieu of the sprint training. In order that the volume of these training forms be safely increased it is, as previously noted, vital that both their inclusion in the yearly training and mechanically efficient performance be secured prior to the time of the shift in load proportionality.

Medium Size Indoor Training Spaces

Regarding indoor training spaces that are large enough provide for max velocity work; but nothing more (i.e. an 80m straight away and crash pads), the only real challenge is solving the problem of speed endurance. We know that special endurance work may be executed via split runs. For this reason, a straight away that is sufficient for max V work is also sufficient for the performance of special endurance split runs. The problem that must be solved is how to achieve a sufficient stimulus in place of speed endurance work.

In actuality, there is no viable alternative for speed endurance sprints that offers a high degree of transfer for a developed sprinter. There are, however, alternatives that may serve as valuable stimulus until the athlete is able to train outdoors.

Similar to the "plan B" strategies relative to sprint alternatives, we may focus our attention on similar, yet not the same, means of stimulating speed endurance adaptations. In this way, we may consider the 8-15 second window of high output exertion and a part whole approach; in which the athletes may perform associated work that possesses similar character in a combination of biomotor + bioenergetic or biodynamic + bioenergetic actions within the available training space.

Short of sprinting, the only way the muscle contractile velocity (biomotor) may be approached is on an exercise bike, such as a spin bike, that allows for high output unlimited human powered cyclic exertion as well the option to adjust resistance. This may be used to approach the biomotor and bioenergetic output aspect of the equation while a running variation may be used to satisfy the biodynamic and bioenergetic aspect of the equation.

Biodynamic + Bioenergetic Solutions

While the biodynamic structure of sprinting is specific to each phase of a sprint, there are sprint drills that may serve as useful alternatives to speed endurance whose biodynamic likeness, while not the same as the structure of speed endurance, is much closer than that of any off the track alternative.

One possibility is resisted sprints with either a sled, or similar, apparatus that the sprinter tows behind them; or a mechanism that provides resistance such as the old Isorobic Exerciser. In this way, it is possible to set a level of resistance that is just enough to slow the sprinter down in such a way that even via their near maximal exertion they are able to work continuously for 8-15 seconds in the given space.

Let us reference Bolt's velocity at the 60m mark in his 9.58 world record performance: we know that his peak velocity was 12.2m/s and his split was 6.29. For the sake of math, however, we'll use the average velocity (d/t) of 9.54m/s. So if the challenge was to see to it that Bolt was able to cover that same distance in 8-15 seconds (let's say 10seconds) we know that his average velocity would have to be decreased to 6m/s. While the neuromuscular output, specifically in reference to muscle contractile velocity, would not be remotely close to that associated with actual speed endurance sprints (and therefore not a viable stand alone alternative), the fact that Bolt would still be attempting to sprint with high intensity satisfies an important biodynamic variable in so far as the movement is a running action.

Alternate leg speed bounds are another viable speed endurance alternative. While the biodynamic structure of speed bounds is distinctly different than sprinting, they are a viable supplement that have stood the test of time in the preparation of many sprinters and speed/power athletes.

Another option for consideration is a modified Running A exercise in which the method of execution is adjusted such that the athlete is moving with high intensity action; yet adjusting their horizontal push off such that it takes them 8-15 seconds to complete the distance.

Reminder that neither the bike option or drill options are viable stand alone alternatives for speed endurance sprints; for any period of time beyond the short term. When combined, however, they may serve to fill an important gap that would otherwise go unsupported for those sprinters whose cold weather training is limited to indoor spaces that do not allow for speed endurance sprints.

IV.2. THERAPY OPTIONS

Sprint training, particularly the training of maximum velocity, ranks as one of the most demanding and intensive forms of training. On average, a short to long approach registers higher in overall training intensity. This is resultant of the fact that a larger overall annual volume of sprints will be conducted at or near the maximum velocity zone in comparison to the long to short approach.

Higher and more frequent training intensity must be met with the necessary therapy to support the demands of the work. Athletes/sprinters who are working on limited budgets, or whose coaches do not possess the time or skills to provide manual therapy, will be challenged to have access to the type and frequency of therapy options that are most well suited for a short to long approach.

IV.3. TOLERANCE TO CNS INTENSIVE LOADING

Every athlete possesses genotypic qualities which, combined with phenotypic factors, determine their tolerance for CNS intensive loading.

Generally, more muscle bound athletes/sprinters possess a higher aptitude for CNS intensive sprint work. Their morphological support structure and typically higher output capacities are more well suited for the stressors associated with the short to long approach. Alternatively, longer/lankier athletes/sprinters will, again generally, respond more favourably to the lesser intensity nature of the long to short method. While the physiological stress is greater the longer the sprint, the neuromuscular stress of the long to short approach is less due to the lesser sum total of annual sprint training volumes conducted in and around the maximal velocity zone.

Ultimately, it becomes a matter of working towards the athletes strengths. All things being equal, and climate, therapy, and tolerances aside, the most logical solution is to stimulate the athlete in a way that is consistent with how they are most receptive to relevant and specific training adaptations. Intrinsic aptitudes suggest greater room for improvement by virtue of the fact that the individual already possesses an innate potential for the work. Further, the task specific nature of the competition event is what determines the task specific nature of the athlete's work capacity developed in training.

IV.4. APPLICATIONS FOR NON-TRACK SPEED/POWER ATHLETES

There are a multitude of pre-existing illustrations of L-S and S-L strategies for track sprinters. Here, we will discuss the implications of L-S and S-L for non-track speed/power athletes regardless if the sport application is team based field or court sport, or pushing the bobsled.

In this realm of sport we know that the vast majority of maximal sprint efforts exist in the domain of acceleration. This amounts to 5-30meters regardless of sport; with the exceptions ranging up to the maximal velocity distances 40-60meters for certain field sports.

If we then extrapolate the premise of L-S and S-L strategies for a non-track speed/power athlete we may place the 30meter distance as the competitive event (as this distance represents the longer end of common lengths over which these athletes will sprint in a competition). No non-track speed/power athlete has a speed or special endurance requirement in their competition demands as there is no instance in which a sprint exertion is sustained continuously for the distances/durations of speed endurance, special endurance I, or special endurance II. There are, however, tremendous applications for these track applications towards many athletes including swimmers, sprint cyclists, and speed skaters.

IV.4.1. LONG TO SHORT FOR NON-TRACK SPEED/POWER ATHLETES

While there is no speed or special endurance requirement for a non-track speed/power athlete, we may effectively utilize special endurance split runs as one means of intelligently using longer and less intensive sprints in the preparation of these athletes as the longer sprint provide a valuable opportunity to enhance rhythm and relaxation which are central to speed development.

Something not as commonly discussed, particularly in the training of non-track athletes, is the value of longer sprints for the purposes of developing the relaxation and rhythmic component of sprint mechanics.

At this point, any coach of a field or court sport athlete might be concerned with the information presented thus far in terms of its relevance towards their purposes. The relief to any possible doubt is rooted in what, at first glance, may not be immediately recognizable regarding the efficacy of a field or court sport athlete performing sprint distances far in excess of any distance they would cover during a competition in an uninterrupted effort.

The significance is rooted in the relaxation, and rhythm, that is associated, by default, with maintaining proper mechanics over longer distances. Nearly any athlete who is faced with sprinting over a distance that is well beyond their competitive requirements will, naturally, self-regulate their output in order to survive the distance/duration of the endeavour. This typically results in enhanced movement economy which is essential for mastering all forms of running; including acceleration mechanics. For this reason, speed endurance and special endurance I efforts are common amongst the training of long jumpers, triple jumpers, vaulters, and high jumpers as rhythm is central to their approach runs.

Alternatively, nearly any non-track athlete who is tasked with sprinting over a short distance will invariably sacrifice movement efficiency for effort. By association, and intrinsically, any untrained person will naturally assume that the harder you try to run the faster you will go; when in fact, nearly the opposite is true. One of the qualities that separates the fastest sprinters in the world from their slower counterparts is their superior ability to exert maximal intensity in concert with maximal relaxation. A paradoxical proposition indeed which no doubt reinforces the fact that sprinting and, by association, acceleration is a skill.

While any number of special endurance distances may be effectively employed for a non-track speed/power athlete, repeat 60meter reps present distinct advantages in that the distance is still moderately specific as the implications on improved 60m sprint speed certainly transfer to a number of team based field sports. In this way, the 60meter reps are initially separated by relatively brief recoveries and utilize intensity limits; both of which serve the purpose of reducing the intensity that would otherwise be even higher.

Additional L-S means for non-track speed/power athletes include longer hill and sled sprints. Both forms of sprinting inherently lessen the neuromuscular intensity of the effort due to the anti-gravitational effort associated with the hill sprint and the greater resistance associated with a sled sprint. In fact, it is equally reasonable to begin at the competition distance, 30m for example in the case of team sport athletes, either on a hill, with a sled, or on flat ground into a head wind, and initiate the work with short rest intervals between reps. In this way, while the actual distance is the same as the competitive requirement, the duration of each effort will be longer which, according to the associated training means, reduces the neuromuscular intensity of the efforts; because in all cases the speed of movement is lessened. All of this would fall under the context of L-S as, over time, either the distance or duration of the sprint efforts would be lessened, along with the increase in recovery intervals between reps, in order to allow for intensification.

IV.4.2. SHORT TO LONG FOR NON-TRACK SPEED/POWER ATHLETES

The short to long approach for the non-track speed/power athlete is more immediately recognizable. The sprint reps, regardless if on a hill, with a sled, or on flat ground will begin shorter than the competitive demands.

5-20 meter sprints are less of a neuromuscular demand than a 30m sprint; provided the athlete(s) are able to continue accelerating over a distance that is equal to or beyond 30meters. Thus, it is effective to begin preparations with these very short accelerations and gradually lengthen the distances, as well as recovery intervals between reps, out to the competitive averages.

In any case, regardless of which approach is used or if the sport is T&F or something else, it is vital to supplement the sprint work with either other supportive sprint efforts (in the case of T&F sprinters who are wise to never get far away from acceleration and pure speed work) or specialized exercises (which positively transfer to the biomotor, biodynamic, and bioenergetic demands of the sport action). Refer to the section on specialized exercises for speed development later in this manual.

IV. 5. A TRACK AND FIELD DISCUSSION

The topic of S-L, L-S, as well as concurrent (a combination of S-L and L-S) approaches have long since occupied the minds of T&F sprint coaches. What is important to point out is that the biggest distinguishing characteristic between all three is nothing more than load proportionality. In this way, the question becomes how might the volume of acceleration, max V, speed endurance, and special endurance be appropriated for each system.

The actual contents of each strategy are nearly identical; save for the special endurance runs that will be performed in either continuous efforts or via split- runs.

The previously listed factors must be considered when it comes time to determine which approach will most optimally serve the sprinters. Some anecdote for your consideration:

- *It has long since been my intuitive as well as experiential knowing that most sport training solutions are solved via a joint coach + athlete effort. I feel that communicative efforts lie at the zenith of importance regarding the joint problem solving venture. It is often this aspect of coach/athlete relationship that fails to manifest itself at the requisite level.*
- *Since the dawn of my coaching/consulting career I have made it a point to establish communication transparency with my athletes. This entails a similarly strategic communicative effort on my behalf as, similar to any other coach with international experience, I have coached and consulted with a vast spectrum of athletes who stem from different cultural/societal/economic as well as linguistic backgrounds. Always seeking to reduce problems down to the basal level it has been my experience that utter honesty is the most prudent course of action. This must be backed by knowledge, however, as even young children possess a bullshit meter.*
- *Transparent communication with athletes must in no way be confused with paralysing them with analysis, however. I view transparent communication as a direct interplay, not instruction, between two or more individuals that, in the sport context, is rooted in formulaic problem*

solving and supported by each individual's aptitude.

- *Formulaic problem solving begins with the complete understanding of the problem itself.*

Let us have a look at the most basal aspects of solving the problem of the 100meters:

- minimize reaction time
- maximize the highest attainable maximum velocity
- stretch the alactic period

The optimization of biomechanics is central towards securing points 2 and 3; therefore, it will be left as a forgone conclusion that mechanical efficiency, in all phases, is a cornerstone of sprint preparation. This is discussed in detail in the applied sciences section.

Basal constituents are unarguable and thus prove integral towards solving problems. If we then consider how we might most effectively assist sprinters in securing these objectives we may take a lesson from something world recognized athletics coach Dan Pfaff has stated regarding how a program has integrity if it you can shrink it or expand it and still benefit from the scheme. We may observe the integrity of the nature of speed development over time and then consider how this same integral process may be adjusted within a single calendar year. In this way, it is reasonable to state that a sprint program for a high level sprinter is neither L-S, concurrent, or S-L; but rather all three.

Initially, a young male sprinter (early teens) will invariably hit their maximum velocity a point that is closer to the blocks then it is the finish line. Then, as the years progress, provided training is optimized, he will extend his ability to hit max V at a point that is farther from the start and closer to the finish.

Females, on the other hand, due to their lesser output ability, must face a more profound output limiter regarding the fact that as their max V develops it will not reach the same speed or distance in the race as a male.

The commonality between the young male and young female sprinter, however, is that both of them will, initially, benefit from a program that is more heavily weighed in L-S tactics. In this way, the greater proportion of the training load will address the aspect of development that will yield the greatest impact on their race results- namely speed endurance and the development of rhythmic qualities.

Then, as the years progress, and the sprinters' increase their maximum velocity the impact of the L-S will lessen; particularly for the male sprinter, as the stimulation generated by the L-S may be insufficient to further develop his maximum velocity. For this reason, he may shift to a concurrent approach in which a greater yearly total of pure speed work is included in the program; yet still balanced by speed endurance and special endurance workloads.

The proportionality shift will be more graded for the female; however, as the speed endurance will forever remain comparatively more essential for her due to the fact that she will never be able to generate the same max V as her male counterparts.

Finally, as the male sprinter reaches international class, he has developed max V in the upper echelon of 11m/s and at this point the lion's share of load proportionality must favour pure speed work. This will be the only stimulus sufficient for raising his max V that much further; even if it is only a fractional improvement.

It is remarkable to note the difference made by even the most fractional improvement in max V.

- Here are Bolt's 10m splits from the 9.58 performance (0-10m does not include his reaction time of .146):

RT	0-10	10-20	20-30	30-40	40-50	50-60	60-70	70-80	80-90	90-100
.146	1.74	.99	.9	.86	.83	.82	.81	.82	.83	.83

- Let us hypothesize that Bolt is capable of the following series of splits which equates to a 9.52:

RT	0-10	10-20	20-30	30-40	40-50	50-60	60-70	70-80	80-90	90-100
.146	1.74	.99	.9	.86	.83	.82	.81	.80	.81	.81

- According to this hypothetical example Bolt would extend the distance of his acceleration to the 80m mark- a difference of 10meters. As he would be falling from a higher speed his speed endurance would also be positively effected and the overall result is an improvement of .06sec. As his max V would be achieved at 80 he would hit the 80m mark at 7.90s.

- The lactic period in the 100m may be stated as the total time minus the time in which the athlete's 10m split increased after hitting max V. In the 9.58 race that happened at the 80m mark. Therefore, we may state that the lactic period in Bolt's 9.58 performance was 1.66sec (9.58-7.92). In this hypothetical 9.52 performance his lactic period would be reduced to .81sec (9.52-8.71) because his 10m split does not increase until the 90m mark. Thus, by shaving off a mere .06 from his total time (.63%), specifically reflective of hitting a higher max V and extending the alactic period, Bolt would reduce the lactic period by an incredible 51%.

The challenge of effectively stimulating a sprinter relative to his or her place in time is the commonality shared between all strategies. The integrity of such a multi-year cycle that works, at least for the male, from L-S to Concurrent to S-L is equally as viable, and commonly practiced, within a single training year. We know this, if for no other reason, because it is essential that a higher volume of pure speed work be introduced prior to the indoor competition season as a pure L-S is insufficient for bolstering 60m results- for an already high level sprinter. More, importantly, however, we know that the stimulation required to advance an elite male sprinter's 100m results can only be found in advancing his maximum velocity.

While the advancement of maximum velocity is equally as important for a female sprinter, the speed endurance is more vital for the female sprinter than it is to the male. For this reason, the proportionality scheme, even regarding two S-L programs, must differ based upon it being applied towards a female or male sprinter.

The biggest question lies in how the special endurance will be executed- via continuous efforts or split runs. Otherwise, it is only sensible that the intensity of the track work performed early in the training year graduate itself towards the competition calendar.

V. TEMPO

Tempo, in the track and field sprint vernacular (specifically the Charlie Francis Training System), represents interval based running sessions in which the sub-maximal intensity of the runs varies based upon whether the nature of the work is extensive or intensive.

V.1. EXTENSIVE TEMPO

Extensive tempo runs are an aerobic endeavour. The aerobic nature of the work is ensured via the established intensity limit of 75% of the athletes max speed for the distance being covered. For example, if a sprinter has a PB of 10.35s for the 100m their 75% intensity for a 100m tempo run would be 13.8 (10.35 divided by .75) . The 13.8 would then be adjusted according to the athlete's training surface. Running on grass, as an example, must be accounted for due to the loss in stiffness, and according force return, during ground support. In this case, one might add an additional .5-1s to the intensity limit which would raise it to 14.3.-14.8sec. In this way, the athlete may run **no faster** than 14.3sec; however any time slower is fine.

It should be noted that it is highly advisable to perform tempo runs on grass whenever possible.

Regarding team based field/court sport athletes, the athletes may run a time trial on the surface in which they will be performing their running training. This will obviate any need to convert the time according to the training surface. It must also be noted that the distance over which the tempo runs are executed is generally associated with the athletes competition event.

- 100/200m sprinters and 100/110m hurdlers will frequently perform tempo runs that are 100-200m in length
- 400m sprinters and hurdlers will typically perform tempo runs that are 100-300m in length
- Team based field and court sport athletes may vary the distance of the tempo runs based upon their competition demands. This is also influence by the size of their competition field/pitch, or court. Additionally, team sport athletes may vary widely in bodymass and this must be

accounted for regarding all running aspects of the training load

- Most team based field sport athletes will perform tempo distances ranging from 40-200m; while football (soccer), rugby backs and sevens, and Aussie Rules Footballers may cover up to 300m per rep.

The topic of total volume per session is both widely debated and contested and there are no right or wrong answers. Observations reveal that 1000-2000meters per session is common for the short sprinters/hurdlers and this volume may increase up to 3000meters per session for a 400m athletes.

Regarding the team sport athletes, the total volume per session must be appropriate relative the aerobic running requirement specific to their competition demands. The following examples are appropriate **upper range** volumes per session for the respective athletes:

- Football (soccer) athletes may cover up to 2500-3000m
- Rugby Union and League Forwards- up to 2000-2500m
- Rugby Union and League Backs and Sevens players- up to 2400-3000m
- American football defensive backs, wide receivers- up to 1600-2000meters
- American football running backs, linebackers- 1200-1600meters
- Basketball players- up to 2000-2500m
- Aussie Rules Football players up to 3000-4000m

while Aussie rules footballers will cover total running volumes per match up to 15-16km, the overwhelming majority of that volume is spent running at very slow speeds <5m/s; which are well beneath the tempo pace that corresponds to those athletes ability. Therefore, any necessary additional aerobic running outside of technical-tactical trainings may be executed in a variety of ways.

V.2. NON-RUNNING TEMPO

Sports such as American football, at the major collegiate and professional levels, will feature offensive and defensive linemen that weigh in excess of 300lbs/~136kg. In a run first pro-style offensive attack, for example, the offensive linemen will perform minimal running per play (5-10yds). In this case, absolutely no aerobic running is required because their competition demand is void of aerobic running.

Volleyball is another example of a team sport that does not necessitate aerobic running in the preparation; and if aerobic running is to be included in the training it is sensible to limit the distances of the intervals to 30-40meters.

In such cases, as well as regarding athletes who may have sustained a leg injury, in the case of prohibitive weather conditions, or regarding the need to develop the oxidative capacity of the arms or legs via special exercises, it will become viable to stress the aerobic system via means other than running. In this way, all that need be satisfied is the bioenergetic intensity limit and sensible work: rest durations of the intervals. If the athlete's anaerobic threshold is known then they may keep their heart rate beneath 100% of the anaerobic threshold.

Cyclical, repeatable, movements lend themselves most readily to tempo variations due to the ease of regulating the working intensity. Common non-running tempo exercises consist of:

- exercise bike
- elliptical
- running in place on an exercise mat
- running in place in the shallow end of a pool
- extensive medicine ball wall rebounds
- power speed schemes
- any variety of calisthenics schemes, circuit training, and resisted arm actions

V.3. INTENSIVE TEMPO

There are instances in which a higher intensity form of tempo may be useful and this domain of tempo is referred to as intensive tempo. The intensive tempo intensity range generally works from 80-85% of the athletes top speed for that distance.

This form of tempo may be useful to enhance lactic capacities for various tasks as well as to serve as a intermediary in a particular running scheme that might progress, over a period of weeks, from extensive tempo to intensive tempo to speed work.

As the neuromuscular and physiological stress of intensive tempo is greater than extensive tempo the total volume per session will be less. The distance/duration of the individual repetitions may be the same as the extensive tempo variety, however.

V. 4. TEMPO VS MAXIMAL AEROBIC SPEED, 300YD SHUTTLE, AND YO-YO

Regarding the preparation of teams based field and court sport athletes whose sport demands necessitate aerobic running fitness, tempo runs present distinct advantages over maximal aerobic speed, the 300yd shuttle (common in the American sports system), Yo-Yo and similar beep test protocols that prevail in many sports organizations around the world.

Important to point out is the fact that the following deconstruction and criticisms of the MAS, 300yd Shuttle, and Yo-Yo are directed towards the low velocity, and frequent poor mechanical nature of the work; not their ability to develop aerobic adaptations.

V.4.1. MAXIMAL AEROBIC SPEED

Maximal aerobic speed training has gained popularity for developing aerobic qualities in team based field sport athletes. The protocols are based upon an aerobic value i.e., an athletes fastest 1.5-2km effort in seconds divided by the distance. This value is then used for interval training set up in such a way that the bioenergetic stress borders on, and often crosses, the lactic threshold due to the brief recoveries (~15sec) that typically separate work bouts of equal duration (~15seconds).

Aerobic MAS intervals are much slower than what an athlete is capable of maintaining in interval fashion, with slightly longer rest periods, while remaining beneath the lactic threshold. Further, the fact that even supra-maximal aerobic speed intervals are relatively slow further diminishes their value as a lactic workload. In a High/Low schedule, the lactic work must be accounted for as a high intensity stimulus and replace, to some degree, a certain volume of high quality alactic speed work.. For this reason, if lactic loading is to replace any amount of alactic loading, the justification is much stronger if the lactic work is of a higher output character.

Keep in mind that most studies show generally the same proportions and low velocity ranges, by track standards, that qualify as 'sprinting' (6-8m/s or so) over 20-30m. Sports such as Rugby Sevens, football (soccer), and the grand master Australian Rules Football surely demand more of aerobic qualities; however, max velocity will ever remain the off setting variable. MAS exists in the medium to low intensity category, depending on the percentage of MAS that is prescribed; though any lactic work, +100% MAS, is not lactic because of intensity, but rather insufficient recovery i.e., 1:1 work: rest intervals. For this reason, this sort of work is a wasted effort for the speed minded individual.

By comparison, special endurance split 60s, lactic accelerations, and even intensive tempo runs, feature terrifically higher velocities while also working in lactic realm. All that said, as Charlie Francis reinforced time and time again, enter the season fit and the game itself will take care of the rest.

- *A practical example may be taken from my tenure with the Portuguese Rugby Federation. During my work their I prepared both national squads, 15s and 7s. One of the 15s players (Goncalo Foro) joined the national Sevens squad for the Dubai and South Africa tournaments in 2012. Goncalo told me that it only took one game for him to acclimate to the pace of the Sevens and at 100kg bodyweight he ran down Hendricks from South Africa during a significant win over South Africa in Dubai. The play is featured in this video at approximately the 13:44 mark:https://www.youtube.com/watch?v=Sc6XmswNWX0*

- *My work with the Portugal Senior National sides included a pure high/low approach in which the athletes performed alactic speed work and extensive tempo. The tempo was performed such that it reached its apex at 3000meters in a session for the backs. The backs would average 15-16seconds per 100m repeats (6.25-6.67m/s). The national sevens coach had an affinity for lactic loading, however, so I made certain adjustments in that, at times, pure alactic speed work was replaced by special endurance split 60meter runs, instead of the Yo-Yo/beep test (another misused training means) runs favored by the coach. The split 60s are far more effective for the game due to the velocities involved.*

MAS achieves it's designated training objective of improved aerobic power through limited regenerative periods separating relatively low intensity running intervals of properly dosed volume. This is one way to toe the line, as well as cross into, the anaerobic threshold and is one means of stimulating aerobic development. The training problem, regarding running, for field sports, however, is not how to solve the problem of aerobic power; it is how to assist the athletes at averaging higher and higher speeds for successive repeats- as the running component in these games does not hinge on "who can repeat the most relatively slow running"; but rather, "who can repeat the highest velocity runs" and support this with sufficient aerobic running economy and capacity.

In speed/power/strength team sports it is logical to recognize the importance of velocity based locomotive efforts and work at either ends of the bioenergetic spectrum (high or low), due to the contribution of more velocity based endeavors towards the vital speed reserve and special work capacity.

In the case of justified methods which approach or include the anaerobic-lactic zone, due to either their aerobic enzymatic and/or speed benefits, it is justified to modify special endurance split runs, intensive tempo runs, as well as lactic acceleration sprints, as the corporate average speeds of those variants substantially exceed Max Aerobic Speed velocities and the bioenergetic manipulation is easily and similarly handled via adjusting rest intervals. It is important to note that, in a high/low scheme, whatever is to be used that falls in the strata between the highest intensities and the 75th percentile must always be accounted for as high intensity. The high/low split is superbly well suited for team sport preparations and will be explained later.

IF speed and aerobic abilities are properly developed. Lactic acceleration, as well as alactic capacity, repeats can allow for 4 or even 6 repeated shorter distance sprint efforts within the alactic period, (which differs based upon each athlete but we'll take 30m as a conservative example) with brief recoveries between reps so long as a full recovery is taken after each set.

By simply watching athletes move- one finds that despite the different work: rest intervals in the various team sport field sports, there is a great deal of standing around, walking around, and low intensity running. The question then becomes, how much of those components actually require <u>ANY</u> preparatory training efforts.

It's all in the math.

Conventionally educated coaches (products of academia) often argue such matters; however, the necessary edification requires no more than visual observation and a timing device.

Consider the current 1500m leader, Asbel Kiprop, who recorded a blazing time of 3:27.72 in July of this past year (2013). His maximal aerobic speed (meters divided by seconds) amounts to 7.22m/s (which would amount to a 13.85sec 100m with a flying start). Kiprop's MAS is phenomenal and well beyond what any field sport athlete in the world is capable of sustaining over 1500m; however, this velocity registers as only 69% of Bolt's average velocity (10.44m/s) and 92% of Bolt's 100m extensive tempo limit.

Extensive tempo parameters dictate that the runs be no faster than 75% of the athletes top speed for that distance. So based upon Bolt's 9.58, at that time, his 100m tempo upper limit would have been 12.77s which equates to an average velocity of 7.83m/s.

So while Kiprop can clearly sustain MAS repeats of 7.22m/s, that time range is 92% of what Bolt can sustain for extensive tempo repeats. While we don't know what Kiprop's max V is, in the alactic period, we would not be delinquent in stating that it is no where near 12.35m/s. So while we similarly do not know Bolt's MAS we have every right to state that if both men were to partake in a game of football (soccer), when the time comes to sprint for a loose ball, well, no speculation required.

Clearly, there are no field sport athletes in the world capable of a 3:27 1500m or a 9.58 100m so we must account for reality- such as an 10.5sec 100m (which would still register as some of the fastest male field sport athletes) and a maximal aerobic speed of 5m/s which would similarly amount to being well above the mark of the corporate average male field sport athletes as it equates to a 5minute 1500m.

While the 10.5sec 100m athlete would hit a peak velocity that is much higher, we may state that his average velocity is 9.52m/s.

Here's the percentage brackets down to 50% for the 10.5sec 100m athlete as well as the supra-maximal percentage brackets for the 5m/s MAS athlete:

10.5m/s		5m/s MAS	
%	m/s	%	m/s
95-100	9.04-9.52	135-140	6.75-7
90-95	8.57-9.04	130-135	6.5-6.75
85-90	8.09-8.57	125-130	6.25-6.5
80-85	7.62-8.09	120-125	6-6.25
75-80	7.14-7.62	115-120	5.75-6
70-75	6.66-7.14	110-115	5.5-5.75
65-70	6.19-6.66	105-110	5.25-5.5
60-65	5.71-6.19	100-105	5-5.25
55-60	5.24-5.71		
50-55	4.76-5.24		

From this table we see that even when the 5m/s MAS athlete is operating at 140% (a profoundly lactic endeavor) he is only touching 73.5% of the 10.5sec 100m athlete's maximal velocity.

The distinction that must be made is that the supra-maximal MAS workload is heavily lactic (due to 1:1 work vs rest) while extensive tempo is aerobic. So the 10.5sec 100m athlete may be covering thousands of meters of extensive tempo at up to 7.14m/s, in addition to the calisthenics that separate the runs, and 20minutes after the session he feels like he hasn't done anything. Meanwhile if the 5m/s MAS athlete were to attempt the 10.5sec 100m athlete's tempo/75% velocity (7.14m/s), at a 1:1 work:rest scheme, he would be operating at 143% MAS (supra-maximal and heavily lactic) and 20minutes later he would probably still be lying on the ground trying to recover.

As to specific sport adaptations of tempo vs MAS, consider the following:
- The 10.5sec 100m athlete has the upper extensive tempo limit of 7.14m/s. Take that compared to a MAS of 5.0m/s (which is 30% slower).

- The 10.5sec 100m athlete, who performs speed and extensive tempo, will enhance both ends of the bioenergetic spectrum and as a result, the realm in between will also be positively affected in terms of the potential. The increased speed increases the reserve as well as the potential to extend upon the alactic capacity and the enhanced aerobic capacity improves the lactate buffer system.

The problem with MAS, in the context of a speed based paradigm, is that it works within the domain of a velocity that is exceedingly sub-maximal to begin with (relative to max V). So while the 5m/s MAS athlete is running his intervals of 15sec with 15sec rests, the 10.5sec 100m athlete is running as fast as 7.14m/s per tempo run and he performs 10-20 pushups or 30-50 abs in between each rep plus an additional 20-30seconds give or take before he does it again.

So the tempo athlete is moving 30% faster and even though he is resting longer his is spreading the work around his entire body via the calisthenics which raises total work capacity. All the while, the tempo athlete is still operating in an aerobic environment because the speed is the 75% percentile, or lower, of his max speed for the distance and the quality of the runs are high- throughout.

Now, let's say special endurance split 60s, lactic accelerations, or intensive tempo runs are being used in place of an alactic power speed session to satisfy a lactic argument. In this case, the differential in velocity is even greater as the 10.5sec 100m athlete is moving at +8.57m/s for the split 60s, slightly less depending on distance for the lactic accelerations, and 7.62-8.09m/s for the intensive tempo, and, while the recoveries are longer than MAS, they are still incomplete.

Even if pure speed work and MAS are being used in conjunction, the speed + tempo athlete presents distinct advantages because he's operating at higher quality levels on both ends and moving faster throughout. Further, the speed + tempo athlete does not have to sacrifice a speed session for a supra-maximal MAS session because his tempo is performed extensively and the training stress is aerobic.

Most male field sport athletes who weigh less than 100kg, and are properly trained, can manage 100m tempo repeats in 15-16sec (hand timed) (6.25-6.67m/s) routinely, over and over and over with pushups and abs in between. Ironically, that m/s range actually qualifies for 'sprint or high intensity running' intensities in most time motion studies which is curious because it's merely extensive tempo for fit athletes.

Disregard the aerobic adaptations for a moment and simply consider velocity and who's max V is higher. Additionally, ask yourself what higher percentage of that max V the athlete can sustain for repeated intervals. As the velocity of the repeats climbs higher and higher, which is the goal, it ceases to be an aerobic quality (provided the recoveries are incomplete). In the middle intensity zone (75-90) it becomes lactic capacity and above that it is an alactic one (as long as the recoveries are lengthened)- alactic capacity (the total work output of the alactic machinery). Higher max velocity ensures higher alactic capacity.

While the MAS athlete may be superior in a 1.5-2km run, the speed + tempo athlete will be victorious in a game of moderate to high speed intervals.

Charlie Francis said it best when he made the analogy of the basketball players who are required to jump over and over despite their poor jumping ability when he said "*having basketball players who can't touch the rim isn't very helpful no matter how many times they can't touch it*".

Thus, a team sport field athlete who struggles to hit 9m/s in a short sprint yet sacrifices valuable speed development reserves on MAS training is merely extending an envelope that isn't fast enough to have an impact.

- *The Sevens players I coached in Portugal, while they had tremendous room for further developments, illustrated this point with the significant wins they had in Dubai and South Africa in 2012; particularly regarding their upset wins over England and South Africa. The Portugal side pulled off the wins in the final seconds of each game. In this way, the athletes' physical capacities could not be ignored.*

MAS supporters for field sports argue that corporate average speeds are effectively maintained, and developed, as a result of the aerobic machinery that is developed via MAS. While this is true, the result is not a difference maker in team field based sports because these sports, while they demand a high level of aerobic fitness, are not contests decided by slow running.

The speed + tempo position states that the aerobic machinery, no matter how well developed, is of secondary importance to maintaining corporate average speeds that are of a higher percentage of higher absolute speeds; because if the max V, or max acceleration ability, is not high enough in the first place then it doesn't matter how many MAS runs are possible regardless of how fast the athlete can't run

Speed reserve is not a stand alone, however, regarding disciplines which require other capacities (be it the 400m in track or a field sport) the value of the reserve is simply the off-shoots of the differentials created and the lessened efforts required to sustain sub-max intensities. This is why the bulk of team sport field athletes should compliment their speed work with aerobic workloads.

The MAS argument is, for all intents and purposes, fine within the context of a method used to proliferate aerobic adaptations; however, the alactic speed + extensive tempo argument states that those adaptations are secondary to the capacity to repeat higher intensity efforts of an alactic nature.

In reference to the significance of perspective, hence the cornerstone of this text being driven by T&F data, we may observe the mediocre, at best, speeds accounted for, and as a result the categories that exist, in the international time: motion research. While the bioenergetic proportionality is different for each field sport, for comparison sake, the fact remains that the primary difference lies in the proportionality itself.

While being able to maintain and repeat anything under 6m/s is highly developable, it pales in comparison to the need of repeated sprint ability (closer percentages to the maximum velocity).

Aerobic adaptations are substantially less restricted by genetic barriers versus qualities to the left of the curve. Thus, one can surely make the argument to work in the direction in which there is most room to improve (i.e., more aerobic and anaerobic-lactic work in favor of alactic speed work); however, not before working backwards from the sport biodynamic/bioenergetic structure. In the case of team based field sports, the time: motion studies reveal they they are largely endeavors of alactic and aerobic efforts (with minimal lactic contribution); and while the aerobic component is proportionally dominant (in terms of volume) in most team based field sports the defining ability of locomotive dominance is not which team can sustain such aerobic velocities throughout the match; rather, which team can sustain the highest percentage of their maximal velocity throughout the match.

Perhaps conventional minds will take more convincing. Further, this discussion has not even touched upon the biggest error in team sport preparation which is the construct of practices themselves. That, however, is a subject that will be left for a separate publication entirely.

As for the comparison, strictly regarding aerobic adaptations, between MAS and tempo varieties, there is no statistical data to make a firm argument for tempo; however, alactic speed work and tempo will always constitute faster running than MAS because even Asbel Kiprop's incredible MAS is just beyond the extensive tempo limit (76%) of the 10.5sec 100m athlete's max velocity.

Another point of distinction, for perspective sake, is to recognize the fact that the lion's share of intervals ran in the team based field sports are well within the alactic distance (<30meters). Thus, while MAS distances cover 15sec of continuous running and the extensive tempo discussed so far has referenced 100m reps, it is of paramount importance to account for the fact that the corporate average distance the team sport field athlete must cover per medium to high intensity locomotive exertion is 10-30meters. This further reinforces the position of a program that prioritizes alactic speed work; as the common distances over which running occurs in the medium, high, and sprint intensities is also within the distance in which the bulk of acceleration occurs for even the worlds fastest sprinters.

In this way, perhaps the most limiting factor is to think only in terms of 'aerobic development'. We must consider it in the context of the sport and even though the aerobic power and capacity are significantly relevant to the various field sport athletes, aerobic training must be kept in perspective. The ultimate examples of the extremes lie in track and field (the truest examples of pure bioenergetic outputs in all of sport) and by comparison, no Rugby man, footballer, or even Aussie Rules Footballer in the world is on par with world class milers or 1500m runners in terms of aerobic power/capacity. In the same way, no field sport player in the world is on par with world class 100m sprinters in terms max velocity (not even Carlin Isles of USA Rugby who is the fastest man in international rugby- by a distance).

Tempo, dosed properly, is more than enough stimulus to meet the aerobic demands of team based field sports with the only debatable exception being Aussie Rules Football. For 1500m runners or milers, absolutely not, however, those middle distance athletes do not have the speed/power requirements of the field sport athlete.

Alactic capacity directly increases the athletes capacity to repeat high intensity sprint efforts;however, as it is linked to alactic ability the plasticity of this realm of improvement is less in magnitude in relation to purely aerobic developments. Interesting enough, however, given the properly dosed loading, the actual ratio between work to rest for alactic capacity can be quite similar to the prescription for MAS; however, the massive difference lies in the intensity of the running which is why, regarding sprint efforts, the number of repeats in a set of alactic capacity work would usually be 4-6 before a larger break is required to prevent the situation from becoming lactic. The work of Zhelyaskov and Dasheva of the NSA in Bulgaria expounds upon bioenergetics in great detail in the Applied Physiology section.

- *My work with the Portugal Sevens, regarding running, consisted only of alactic power, tempo, and spec end split 60s (because of the limited relevance of the yo-yo test so I convinced the head coach to allow me to conduct the split 60s instead for many of the same reasons that I've discussed here). Anecdotally, my Sevens player said they felt that they were more fit, as well as physically stronger, than many of the teams they faced after only 8 weeks of restructured training via a high/low framework.*

As for the VO2max concepts linked to the MAS protocols, the significance of VO2max was dismissed decades ago by the Russians, namely Verkhoshansky, who described how the elite of the elite (in endurance sports) actually demonstrated a decline in VO2 max over the years due to increased movement efficiency. Further, he went on to describe that the oxidative potential of the muscles (the anaerobic threshold), a local process, is the true determinant- hence the need for specific preparation even in the aerobic sense.

So while aerobic running covers the specificity of oxidative muscle function for running, there are a myriad of specific movements which cover the demands for the combative and multi-directional movement demands of the various field sports.

There is no argument against the fact that MAS will develop aerobic qualities and raise the lactic threshold; however, why limit the true ceiling, max velocity, (at any possible chance to raise it) in favor of working in the basement?

While it is pertinent to state that the development of the aerobic system is essential for the team based field sports, it is equally pertinent to state that MAS training can inappropriately become lactic in the race to out work the opposition. Alternatively, adjustments to MAS loading, so that it remains aerobic, are much closer to tempo, other than how much slower it is, because the only strict guidelines for tempo are the ceiling of intensity and the requirement to execute all repeats without a loss in speed or increased effort to execute the same speed. Therein lies the difference, if MAS is to be executed via progressively more challenging loading then it must be placed on a high intensity training day due to the lactic component.

Tempo is sub-max to begin with, and the more sub-max it is the lesser the neuromuscular intensity; alternatively , the higher the max V, the faster the tempo while still remaining sub-max as it's always relative to each athlete's maximum (same for increased MAS and its percentages, however the race to increase the speed of the intervals, to what amounts to middle distance speed, is counterintuitive for the field sport athlete.)

What most camps will agree upon is that the most important aspect of running is the ability to repeat the highest possible intensity over the course of the game. The MAS model wants to approach it from the bottom up and sprint + tempo model works from the top down in so far as the objective is directed towards increased speed and the associated speed reserve.

When things become interesting is when the MAS supporters seek to work within the High/Low framework and essentially substitute tempo with modified (lower intensity MAS) which is dangerously approaching the semantic realm as the line between the optimal loading of MAS and the flexibility of tempo is very thin.

V.4.2. 300YD SHUTTLE

The 300yd shuttle is a virtual staple in the repertoire of many team sport conditioning coaches in the United States. Much to the misfortunate of their athletes, however, is the fact that that the structure of this physical endeavour bares minimal, if not negative, relevance towards team sport demands.

Perhaps the most common variant of the test is as its performed in the American football realm. In this way, the athletes are required to run from the goal line to the 25yd line and back 6 times- for a total of 300yds. Over the years, certain time ranges have been designated for the various positions. The required times typically vary between 55 and 60 seconds- depending on position.

Problematically, not unlike supra-maximal MAS protocols, the 300yd shuttle is an anaerobic-lactic endeavour characterized by low outputs. For this reason, it also poses problems regarding recovery and the placement of vital alactic speed work in a training week. The middle intensity zone, in which the 300yd shuttle exists, falls within the heading "too slow to develop speed and too fast to recover from in 24 hours".

Like many other lactic protocols, the gruelling nature of the shuttle, particularly regarding the performance of a a series of repetitions, plays towards the misguided interests of many coaches who fail to recognize the actual bioenergetic structure of sport. Further, the fact that the endeavour is a shuttle performed over a relatively large total distance, via very short intervals, and for a total time that is well beyond what allows for higher velocities- prohibits the speed of movement. Thus, from a speed minded perspective, the 300yd shuttle fails on multiple levels. Not only does it bare no relation to the bioenergetic structure of most team sports (which are alactic-aerobic), and pose programming challenges in a training week when speed training is meant to be included, it also limits output potential.

Therefore let it be recognized that if one's goal is to generate unrelated training adaptation while potentially retarding speed development then consider 300yd shuttles a job well done.

V.4.3. THE YO-YO TEST

The Yo-Yo test/training, is a beep test of repeated 20m intervals, separated by minimal recoveries, that increase in speed on successive attempts. The test is widely used as a training protocol and its popularity in this regard spans the globe. The anaerobic-lactic eventuality of it, similar to supra-maximal MAS training and the 300yd shuttle, however, then competes with the number of available alactic speed sessions per week. Further, the sum total of work performed, of a high velocity character, during the Yo-Yo pales in comparison to the corporate average speeds covered in extensive tempo and is fantastically slower than intensive tempo, lactic accelerations, and ultimately split 60m spec endurance IF the choice is made to involve lactic loads in place of an alactic session.

Thus, while the MAS, 300yd shuttle, and Yo-Yo protocols accomplish the task of stressing aerobic development/maximal oxygen uptake capacity the real question is what is the relevance of these protocols in comparison to the approach that favours a speed based program supplemented by aerobic workloads in the form of extensive tempo.

A more favourable alternative for coaches who are incurably addicted to subjecting their athletes to misappropriated means of lactic running are special endurance split runs as well as lactic starts/short sprints. In this way, the attainable sprint velocities are exceedingly greater than the MAS, 300yd shuttle and Yo-Yo intervals as the distances of the repeats will be set at acceleration ranges or the mark in which the respective athletes are able to hit their maximum velocity (even though they will not achieve their true max V during these sessions due to fatigue).

World renown athletics coach Dan Pfaff has expounded upon this regarding his experience in having sprinters perform block starts, say out to 30m, in which the recoveries between efforts are incomplete. In this way, the bioenergetic stress yields aerobic/enzymatic adaptations similar to aerobic loading; yet in a much shorter time period via actual methods of execution that are much higher in velocity.

This approach to aerobic development, via more specific means of execution, is absolutely justified in sport endeavours in which there is no aerobic running requirement. It just so happens to be, however, that the vast majority, but not all, of team sports require a moderate to high level of aerobic fitness as is demonstrated via running. For this reason, coaches and athletes whose sports/positions demand aerobic running fitness must take a close look at the most appropriate means of its development within the framework of a schedule that involves speed work. This is stated specifically because there is more to aerobic development then what occurs in the general sense; the aerobic development is only as useful as the improved oxidative potential of the muscles involved in the work in addition to the enhanced biomechanical efficiency of the action that is executed at an aerobic intensity.

VI. THE UTILITY OF POWER SPEED

Power speed drills are recognized in T&F circles as exercises which incorporate a kinematic likeness towards the sprint action. They are frequently found in many sprinters' warm up routines.Their degree of direct transfer towards sprinting may be limited, however, due to the absence of neuromuscular similarity; in so far as the drills are not, and cannot, be performed at movement velocities or muscle contraction velocities that even begin to approach those associated with the sprint action; particularly the maximal and near maximal velocity realm.

The utility of these drills, including the thematic transferability for many different athletes' competitive demands, must not be underestimated, however.

VI.1. THE DRILLS

There are dozens of exercises, and variations, that qualify as power speed in the context of sprint preparation. When the context is shifted to athletes who compete in any number of other sports the number of possibilities increases dramatically.

As with all preparatory movements, the context is defined by the specific structure of the competition action. Thus, regarding the sprint development applications, some of the more common drills are as follows:

- A Skips
- Lateral Skips
- Backward Skips
- Running A's (high knees)
    - Double, single, or alternating leg
- B Skips
- Running B's
    - Double, single, or alternating leg

- C Skips
- Bum Kicks
    - Double, single, or alternating leg
- Scissor Bounds/Stiff Leg Dollies
- Any number of double, single, and alternative leg hops
- Backward Runs
- and more...

The movement possibilities are expanded when the context of power speed is shifted towards the specific competition manoeuvres of athletes competing in any number of team based field or court sports or combative sports. In this way, any number of locomotive, cyclic, and acyclic movements (including drills for the arms) are viable options. The only guidelines are that the movements possess, at minimum, a kinematic relationship towards the competition manoeuvre, that the execution of the drills emphasize rhythm and relaxation, and that the work is sub-maximal/low intensive enough to allow for high volumes of work to performed; even on successive days.

VI.2. WARM UP- READINESS ASSESSMENT

Power speed drills are most commonly found as a part of a sprinter's warm up routine. In this way, the drills are typically performed after a general warm up has been initiated that serves to raise general body temperature as well as specific intramuscular temperature and promote joint mobility. Once these prerequisites are in place the athlete is more favourably prepared for the movement dynamics associated with the power speed drills.

It is useful, regarding warm up purposes, to ensure that the drills are executed in a sub-maximal alactic or aerobic, but not lactic, environment. In this way, the drills may be performed over shorter distances at slightly higher movement intensities or longer distances via lesser movement intensities. Refer to the table featuring bioenergetic training parameters in the Applied Physiology section for details. In either case, the physiological expense is low enough to prime and not hinder the subsequent training activities.

What is of paramount importance is that the coach take advantage of this time, as well as any other, to observe the athlete's movement mechanics; as their movement characteristics pose direct implications on their readiness in that moment.

The various power speed drills, regardless if they directed towards linear sprint or multi-dimensional team/field/court/combat sports, will, by nature, involve reactive/elastic movement qualities. In this, the coach is able to assess the state of the athletes neuromuscular readiness based upon the evaluation of various biomotor qualities such as fluidity and timing. If the drill is locomotive in nature than the way in which the athlete's feet make contact with the ground, in terms of sound as well as elastic response/ground contact time, may serve as a useful indicator. Provided the athlete is well trained, heavy footedness, unintentionally delayed ground contact times, as well as lack of coordination/lethargic movement, are all indicators that the athlete is operating in a state of undesirable neuromuscular fatigue.

VI.3. MOVEMENT ENHANCEMENT

The nature via which any conceivable power speed drill is performed is an excellent opportunity to enhance movement. This is so because rhythm and relaxation are central towards the execution of any power speed drill. Thus, no matter whether the power speed is realized via skips and bum kicks or a positional manoeuvre that corresponds to a field or court sport athlete's competition demands, the methods of execution must demonstrate rhythm and relaxation in common.

The sub-maximal intensity of the work lends itself to frequent performance and in relatively high volumes. Two factors that are intrinsic to motor skill development.

VI.4. TEMPO ALTERNATIVE

Individuals already familiar with tempo work understand how the exercise may become monotonous. Adjusting the method of execution of various power speed drills is a viable alternative.

In this way, any power speed drill is modified to be performed extensively such that it may be performed over a far greater distance than what is typical; in an aerobic bioenergetic environment. A sprinter might select to perform A skips for 50-100m lengths whereas a basketball player or American football linebacker might select to perform lateral runs or shuffles. The only guidelines are that the efforts: remain aerobic, are performed in interval fashion, and the movements be executed with efficiency.

VI.5. REHABILITATION

Misinformation permeates the academic curricula of aspiring sports professionals in the domains of physical preparation and rehabilitation alike. Consequently, the steps taken during muscle pull rehabilitation are often void of attention paid towards kinematic and neuromuscular factors.

Hamstring rehab is a classic example. Typically, the fundamental constituents of hamstring rehab will consist of sub-max lengthening hamstring curls along with other tonic strength exercises; because the false positive of a post hamstring pull assessment is a "weakness." This is curious because this suggests that the strength that existed just prior to the pull has disappeared.

What actually happens is that a pull, depending on severity, will at the least, cause certain fibers to go into spasm, or at the most involve tearing, and to different degrees, of certain fibers. In both cases, however, spasm occurs to the surrounding fibers and when fiber is in spasm it cannot contract.

The perceived weakness is actually fibers that are impaired from contracting. If, particularly regarding pulls in which substantial tearing occurs, hands on therapy is not performed the scar tissue will form asynchronously related to the direction of the muscle fiber. This is why massage critical to the rehabilitation and training process in general.

The scar tissue forms haphazardly. Picture a bed sheet that has a hole torn in it. If you sew a patch in the hole and then stretch the sheet, the stress will be focused along the perimeter of the patch where it connects with the threads of the sheet and this is where future tears are likely to occur.

Muscle fiber behaves similarly. It is critical that the fibers of the scar tissue form in the same direction as the muscle fiber. In this way, the future stress of training will be naturally distributed along the fiber and not localized to the haphazard formation of untreated scar tissue.

As for physical training, it is futile to address hamstring rehab solely via tonic strength exercise because the neuromuscular dynamics aren't remotely close to those associated with the dynamics of hamstring contraction via sprinting.

This is where power speed drills and short sub-max accelerations come into play. It is critical to condition the hamstrings via efforts that possess a neuromuscular similarity to that which constitutes the athletes primary responsibility- medium to high speed terrestrial locomotive efforts.

Power speed exercises such as A skips and Running A's involve kinematics that are similar to sprinting and, while the muscle contractile velocity is much slower, the movements still provide the critical reactive/elastic challenges to the muscle-tendon complex while presenting minimal stress to the hamstrings. This has been established via personal experience, the work of Gerard Mach, the late Charlie Francis, and Derek Hansen at Simon Frazier University in Vancouver.

VII. TASK SPECIFIC WORK CAPACITY

This is where many antiquated training myths are readily debunked. Historically, in a variety of disciplines (particularly cyclical endeavours such as track events, swimming, cycling, skating, canoe...) coaches will begin off-season preparations with 'base' training. As world recognized athletics coach Dan Pfaff has stated on more than one occasion "a base of what?"

Indeed

What the athlete spends the greatest proportional amount of time doing in training is what constitutes the 'base' of work capacity. For this reason, if the greatest proportion of training volume is spent on work demands that differ greatly from the competition demands, then the work capacity that has been developed has little relevance to the competition requirements. Surely, this sounds intuitive; however, this logical way of thinking has eluded coaches through the ages.

The 'base' training that so many cyclic athletes are familiar with is characterized by volumes of work that are low in intensity and long in duration. In reality, however, the only disciplines in which this sort of work actually serves as a base for are disciplines that are rooted in low intensity and long duration work efforts. What so many coaches and athletes fail to realize is that this sort of training is prohibitive to advancing every athlete's preparation who competes in event disciplines that are higher in intensity and shorter in duration. This holds true even if the misdirected 'base' training only takes place for a few weeks. No competitive athlete has a long enough off-season to justify time wasted.

Track and swimming athletes are arguably the ones most negatively affected by these damaging workloads. Not only do long/slow efforts have little relevance for track or swim sprinters, they also contribute to far greater repetitive motion stress.

The long to short and short to long approaches, as well as aggregates of the two, all provide for new training years to begin with lesser intensity efforts.

- In the L-S this is done through continuous special endurance I and II runs
- In the S-L this is done through special endurance split runs

While the S-L version of split runs are more CNS intensive than the continuous special endurance I and II runs in the L-S, the intensity is kept sub-maximal due to, what begins as, substantially incomplete recoveries between the reps as well as intensity limits being set which reduce the distance over which the athlete must accelerate.

The training intensity builds over time regardless of which approach is employed:
- In the L-S because the runs become shorter, progressing from special endurance II to I and finally into the speed endurance zone, and the recoveries between them become greater
- In the S-L because the recoveries between the split reps become full such that the training load shifts from special endurance to maximum velocity

As a reminder, all forms of sprint training are present no matter which methodological approach is used. It is the supplementary volume of the training load that is made up for and fortified with the aspects of sprint work that do not constitute to the primary emphasis earlier in the annual preparation (starts, accelerations, max velocity, and speed endurance). Then, as the competition calendar approaches, the aspect of the training load that constitutes the emphasis shifts to the most specific requirement, which for the 100/200m sprinter, is maximum velocity and speed endurance. In this way, what began as supplementary workloads shift to primary workloads and what began as the primary workload (special endurance training) shifts to supplementary workloads.

This shifting of the proportionality and contribution of the workload contents is the basis for what will be discussed as being the next evolutionary step in sports training load management (regardless of sport). In the beginning of the training year the kinematic similarity, not equivalent, but similarity is present while the neuromuscular similarity is reduced. Meanwhile, the additional training elements remain present yet performed at lesser intensities. The degree of separation between the two lessens and lessons over time until the proportions invert and the graduated slope of intensification of the most specific work continues seamlessly while the training load continues to be fortified with the other essential aspects of work.

VIII. IMPLICATIONS ON SPORT TRAINING LOAD MANAGEMENT

Charlie Francis fully elaborated upon the nature of the L-S and S-L systems in many of his writings and lectures. Here, important take aways on each will be discussed as well as the paradigm shifting implications and potential of Charlie's work towards the revolution of sport training load management.

While the general theme of each method is delineated by the distances covered in the stages of preparation, the supposition lies in the proportionality and contribution of the different forms of sprint training and the transferable analogies which extend from their discussion.

In either approach, for a large part of the preparatory stage, the primary contributor to the overall training load volume is special endurance work. In this way, the special endurance reps serve as the training element that prepares the sprinter for the stress of the task specific work capacity for the competition demand which precedes the competition period (max velocity and speed endurance training). The difference is that in a long to short it is standard to perform continuous reps in the special endurance I and II domains and in a short to long it is standard to perform split runs such that a single special endurance I or II rep is subdivided into two or more segments separated by specific rest intervals. The rest intervals begin shorter to limit the attainable intensity of the runs and as time moves forward the rest intervals increase to allow for intensification.

In neither case may the athlete make a living on the special endurance alone, however. The training must be supplemented with the vital start, acceleration, and maximum velocity work; otherwise, the overall training load volume would become too small and lack in fortification by the time the competition calendar arrived. This is the pitfall of any pure linear model of progressive overload.

The inverse relationship between volume and intensity is essentially only pertinent to the most intensive training load elements; not the entirety of training load elements. In this way, one may think of the relationship between the special endurance loading and all other sprint work:

- while the overall volume and intensity progresses in inverse proportions, the remainder of secondary/supportive/auxiliary... training load elements must remain ever present in supplementary volumes to provide the essential fortification/dimensionality to the training load.

Task specific work capacity is a fundamental requirement for any athlete. It signifies the capacity to perform work that is competition/event specific. Regarding a short sprinter, the development of task specific work capacity cannot be limited to special endurance alone; or any other single form of sprint work. This is because as the intensity of any single aspect of sprint work rises, as it will over time, the volume must decrease. Thus, if the training were to be irresponsibly limited to only one form of training (ergo only special endurance, or only max velocity, or only acceleration...) by the time the competition calendar arrived the overall training load will have become too small to effectively sustain peaking ability for successive contests.

- *As an aside, this is one of the premises for the development of the Block Training System; however, it it is my opinion that it is not suitable for the preparation of a sprinter due to the risk associated with concentrated load magnitude of maximum velocity sprinting.*

Thus, regardless of what the sprinter is making their living on (long to short, short to long, or a combined approach) the primary training load contribution must be supplemented by the other essential contributing factors; which, for a sprinter, are the start, acceleration, and maximum velocity work.

Therein lies the revolutionary takeaway for coaches in any other sport...to consider the specific practice of the competition exercise over the term of an off-season and approach the competition calendar from either a long to short, combined, or short to long plan of attack. In this way, the loading of the competition exercise training will be adjusted to begin an off-season with lesser intensity neuromuscular workloads that still retain kinematic transference and gradually increase the intensity of the neuromuscular loading as the competition calendar approaches. Simultaneously, the load will be fortified with training that allows for higher intensity neuromuscular efforts in the form of specialized developmental, preparatory, and general workloads (see the work of Anatoliy Bondarchuk for explanations of these terms).

IX. ACCELERATION IS A SKILL

Coaches outside of the T&F realm are often challenged to accept the reality that acceleration is a skill. In fact, from a neuromuscular standpoint, it is one of the most complex skills for an athlete to master. This is rooted in the optimization of mechanics, development of muscular contraction velocities, as well as intricately timed relaxation requirements of antagonistic musculature that are associated with higher and higher sprint speeds.

It is natural for one to consider the fine motor skill associated with mastering a golf swing, or a tennis serve, or fencing and the corresponding years of training required to develop mastery in those and other disciplines. By contrast, to many, sprinting is associated with a natural/biological occurring activity for all humans. It is here where a distinction must be made, if for no other reason than the sake of explanation, between running fast and sprinting.

Anyone, regardless of training, can run fast relative to their individual ability. No one, however, can sprint well without proper training. While any high level sprinter's actions seem accessible to the observer (starting explosively, accelerating aggressively, transitioning smoothly to the upright position, maintaining rhythm and relaxation through the finish...) it is another thing entirely to be able to execute these actions with efficiency. More on this in the Applied Biomechanics section.

Further, the optimization of running mechanics not only enhances acceleration and all facets of sprint ability, it will also vastly reduce the epidemic of non-contact related injuries that plague pre-competition trainings around the world.

X. REDUCTION OF NON-CONTACT INJURY

If mismanaged training loads are the number one cause of non-contact injury, then inefficient movement mechanics are its identical twin.

It has been previously mentioned that movement is the commonality shared between all sports and sprint/acceleration ability is common denominator between all sprint, jump, field, or court sport disciplines. Not only must we accept the fact that all of these athletes share sprinting in common, we must also recognize that in nearly all cases, it is the activity that they do most. In fact, one would not be remiss in stating that any sprinter, jumper, field, or court sport athlete's discipline is based upon sprinting and_____ (insert the movement forms which characterize the sports technical manoeuvres).

The optimization of sprint mechanics is essential and it is inexcusable to omit acceleration development from the training of any athlete whose sport demands it.

We know that the fastest sprinting registers as one of the most neuromuscular as well as structurally stressful forms of training. When coupled with the fact that acceleration is the movement commonality shared between all sprint, jump, field, and court sport disciplines then it is clear that its optimization is essential for minimizing the training stress.

Consider the volume of running in general that is associated with both the training as well as competition demands of sprinters, jumpers, field, and court sport athletes. Don't make the mistake of accounting for the volume in meters, yards, kilometres, or miles, however. For the purposes of this argument we must consider the volume in steps/strides as every step taken represents a contact/impact with the ground and as the running speed increases so do the impact forces.

From a sprint training perspective, it is not uncommon for a 100m sprinter to perform 600-700 meters of work in a single training session that includes speed or special endurance runs. Race data reveals that many of the fastest 100m sprinters cover the distance in 41 to 46 strides (while their speeds, and corresponding force outputs, are comparable the biggest determining factor is their anthropometry). Taking this into account it is not unreasonable to estimate that one of these same sprinters performing a sprint session that includes speed endurance work might total in the range of several hundreds of ground contacts in a single session.

If we then extrapolate this data to a competition for a field or court sport athlete we know that we must first account for lesser ground impact forces, and subsequent small stride lengths, due to their lesser speed potential; however, the likelihood is much greater that the volume of ground contacts will increase astronomically.

For example, various sport statistical resources agree that in field sports such as Rugby Union it is not uncommon for those athletes to total 5-7km of running per match (depending on position and tactics) and in Australian rules football, the mother of all field based sports in terms of running volumes, the totals may climb as high as 12-13km in a single match (these numbers were almost double in years past prior to the increased frequency of rotating players in and out of a match).

Cornerbacks and wideouts in American football may cover up to 1.25miles or right around 2km per game.

NBA players may average between 2 and 2.5miles per game or 3.2 to 4km

Tennis players in a full 5 set match may cover between 3 and 5miles or 4.8 to 8km.

In terms of ground impacts, resultant of running, and depending on the sport in question, we are now looking at close to a thousand of ground contact repetitions in a single American football game (small skill players) up to several thousand for an Aussie Rules footballer.

These figures merely represent the volumes of ground contacts that occur during a **single contest** and surely the movement speed is highly variable in all field and court sports. That being said, we must further account for the galactic volume increase when we begin adding up daily, weekly, monthly... training sessions.

When discussed in such terms- any coach must then ask themselves the following question: what price does each athlete pay every time their foot hits the ground in an inefficient manner? The answer to this question should make clear the fact that an inordinate amount of non-contact injuries, particularly sustained to the low back, hips, legs, knees, ankles, and feet, regardless of sport, may be attributed to inefficient running mechanics. There is no sport conducted on a track, field/pitch, or court that includes volumes of repetitive movement based tasks that come even remotely close to the volume of running. It is therefore this aspect of track, field/pitch, and court sport preparation that must be placed at the forefront of mechanical development as well as strategic loading.

X.1. HAMSTRINGS AS A BAROMETER OF TRAINING LOAD MANAGEMENT

Regarding the preparation of speed/power athletes, the state of the athletes' hamstring health is arguably the most viable barometer for the coaches ability to manage the training load. The hamstrings are central towards sprint efforts in the upright position and the muscle contractile velocities at the moment of co-contraction prior to foot strike are phenomenal at maximum velocity.

Hamstring pulls, as only one example of common and often avoidable non-contact muscular trauma, are typically written off as an eventuality of hard training. Far more accurately, however, would be to state that hamstring pulls, in the event that the athletes are mechanically efficient in sprinting, are an eventuality of a mismanaged training load.

Key performance indicators (KPI's) are a standard of high performance sports management. Perhaps a new acronym might work its way into the high performance vernacular (KII's) 'key incompetence indicators'. In this way, as the KII's surpass a reasonable number there is no question as to who is responsible. KII's would include a spectrum of non-contact muscular and connective tissue traumas that plague the sports world.

While the mismanagement of training load is a majority share holder in the business of avoidable sports injuries, it would be inaccurate to state that all non-contact injuries are avoidable.

Either way, in the case of muscle pulls, there are certain protocols to follow relative to the severity of structural deformation.

Using the hamstrings as an example we may consider the gradation of pull (1, 2, or 3). Different resources suggest different qualifiers regarding the grading system. Ultimately, diagnostic images such as MRI provide the most accuracy regarding the degree of structural damage. In any case, grade 1 is the least severe and grade 3 is the most severe.

In a grade three tear the degree of tissue deformation is substantial and may very well be visible. This is the least common of the three grades regarding hamstring related sports injury.

A grade two tear presents less substantial tissue deformation; however, manual palpation will typically reveal the deformity.

A grade one tear will not reveal itself in a hands on examination as the degree of tissue damage is minor.

Bruising around the affected area may present itself in all three cases; certainly in the case of grade two and three tears.

The rehabilitation section specific to the applications of power speed shed light on the validity of power speed and modified acceleration work in the rehab process. Here we will go into some detail regarding the big picture thought process that is essential to managing rehabilitation- using the hamstrings as an example.

We previously established the significance of stimulating the muscles in such a way that corresponds more closely to the biodynamic structure of sprinting. In this way, a variety of power speed and modified sprint drills prove themselves as essential training elements. The modifications are made based upon the severity of the pull.

Basal constituents:

- What can the athlete tolerate?
- The hamstrings sustain the load of the athlete's bodymass during ground contact
- The hamstrings are at their most lengthened state during toe off
- If the tear is proximal the athlete will typically have difficulty tolerating knee lift
- If the tear is distal the athlete will typically have difficulty tolerating knee extension prior to ground contact as the hamstrings undergo more rapid lengthening at that point
- At the moment of ground contact and as the hips travel over the foot the hamstrings incur substantial loading

Following are logical movement progressions that I have used in my own coaching and consulting practices for locomotive rehabilitation that do not include actual sprinting (provided each action is tolerable the performance of each one will prepare the athlete for the subsequent action):

1. A March- Walking Up Hill, Stadium Stairs, or on the Flat

Lateral March	Forward March

2. A Skip Up Hill or Up Stadium Stairs
   - Low intensity small stride length
   - Higher intensity small stride length
   - Low intensity increasing stride length
   - Higher intensity increasing stride length

Lateral Skip   Forward Skip

3. A Skip on the Flat

    •   Low intensity increasing stride length

    •   Higher intensity increasing stride length

Small Stride Length   Higher Intensity- Longer Stride Length
Note the Vertical Posture   Note the Angle of Extension

4. A Run (High Knees) Up Hill or Up Stadium Stairs

    •   Graduate the intensity according to tolerance

5. A Run (High Knees) on the Flat

    •   Graduate the intensity according to tolerance

*Note that the B series (March, Skip, Run) are viable actions to be used in such a process; however, most athletes outside of the T&F realm are not proficient in these actions and the process of rehabilitation is not the time to learn them.

Both the march and run variations (A and B) may be performed single leg in which the affected leg remains extended. This form of single leg drill work is usually tolerable within the closest proximity to the time of injury. Additionally, a variety of drills forms performed in the shallow end of a pool are highly useful rehabilitation modalities (due to the reduced anti-gravitational forces) and equally as tolerable close to the time of injury.

If the A Run is tolerable then the athlete will near the point of tolerating very short acceleration sprints- ideally initiated on a hill or stairs in order to further reduce ground impact force. The shorter the distance the less the involvement of the hamstrings. Progressions build from as short as 5m and may work in 5m increments out to 20 or 30m depending on the athlete and tolerance.

In all cases, tolerance dictates loading and scheme. There are no absolutes as to volumes of work to be performed per unit of time. There is an arguable 'dose paradox' that exists in the domain of rehabilitation in which there is justification for seeking the, counterintuitive, maximum effective dose.

Rehabilitation is nothing more than re-establishing load tolerance for, ultimately, the competition action. The process of re-establishing load tolerance demands extensive work and in order to re-form the vital task specific work capacity the volume of work must be substantial; yet strategically managed. As there are no definitive load parameters for rehabilitative measures it the responsibility of the coach and athlete to maintain transparent communication. This ensures synergy between the processes of instruction, execution, and results.

XI. TRAINABILITY OF SPEED

Speed training, outside of the realm of T&F, is surrounded by an astonishing degree of misinformation. A multitude of non-T&F coaches operate under the belief that "you can't teach speed". While it is true that sprint speed potential is heavily dependent upon genetically passed on material from one's progenitors, it is equally true that the concept of "you can't teach speed" is entirely false.

A chronological examination of 7 of the fastest sprinters the world have ever known is all the evidence one needs to illustrate this point. While speed improvement is not linear from one evaluation to the next, the improvements over time, provided the training is optimized and the athletes remain healthy, clearly demonstrate continued evolution up until the point the life time personal best is achieved: (data compiled from IAAF records and information shared from the late Charlie Francis)

Year	Yohan Blake 200m	Yohan Blake 100m	Usain Bolt 200m	Usain Bolt 100m	Asafa Powell 200m	Asafa Powell 100m	Tyson Gay 200m	Tyson Gay 100m	Maurice Greene 100m	Carl Lewis 100m	Ben Johnson 100m
2012		9.69									
2011	19.26	9.82									
2010	19.78	9.89									
2009	20.60	9.93	19.19	9.58			19.58	9.69			
2008	21.06	10.27	19.30	9.69		9.72	**20.00**	9.77			
2007	20.62	10.11	19.75	10.03		9.77	19.62	9.84			
2006	20.92	10.33	19.88		19.90	9.77	19.68	9.84			
2005		10.56	19.99			9.77	19.93	10.08			
2004			19.93		20.06	9.87	20.07	10.06			
2003			20.13			10.02					
2002			20.58		20.48	10.12	20.88	10.27			
2001			21.73					10.28			
2000											
1999									9.79		
1998									9.90		
1997									9.86		
1996									10.08		
1995									10.19		
1994											
1993									10.43		
1992											
1991											
1990											
1989											
1988										9.92	9.79
1987										9.93	9.83
1986											9.95
1985										9.98	10.00
1984										9.99	10.12
1983										9.97	10.19
1982										10.00	10.30
1981										10.00	10.25
1980											10.62
1979											10.66
1978											10.79
1977											11.5

The 20.00 ran by Tyson Gay in 2008 was subsequent to a major hamstring injury. Hence the dramatic difference between it and his best times in the adjacent years.

The review of this data, as well as any other sprinter's results over time leading up to their personal best, reveals improved speed (measured via diagnostic devices much more reliable than hand held stopwatches). Thus, if the world's fastest sprinters are capable of developing their speed it must be recognized once and for all that so can anyone else; and regarding team sports, the value of improved sprint speed is profound.

This section would be incomplete without presenting a valid counter argument which states that these T&F sprinters are predominantly demonstrating improvements in the latter stages of the race (after the zone of primary acceleration); and the majority of non-T&F sprint dependent athletes rely upon short acceleration, not maximum velocity and speed endurance. Thus, one would not be incorrect in stating that a 100/200m who is capable of showing continued improvements past the initial zone of acceleration bares no real significance to an athlete who makes a living on short acceleration; which by comparison, has less room for improvement.

Not so fast...

That statement could only be valid if the non-T&F sprint dependent athletes were already maximizing their potential to develop acceleration qualities. This is not the case, however. In order to maximize acceleration qualities every athlete who depends on it would have to be exposed to levels of both global training load management and biomechanical instruction that are the unicorns of the sports world.

XI.1. THE VALUE OF SPEED FOR TEAM SPORT ATHLETES

Team sports are characterized by intervals of work. The intermittent nature of work performed is representative of a mixed motor regime structure; a large portion of which is constituted by sprint efforts.

Time: Motion research conducted on a variety of team sports illustrates the various running forms (jogging, striding, medium intensity, high intensity, sprinting, ...) and their proportionality and contribution to competitions. A close review of this data reveals the corporate average speeds that are recorded relative to the regime of running.

Logic dictates that all interval based efforts beyond jogging, regarding speed/power team/field sports, should be compared to the maximum of alactic speed, not maximum of aerobic speed as is often done in teams based field sports, in order to establish a percentage based framework of bioenergetic stress.

Consider the following graph which illustrates Bolt's 20m (10.1)and 30m (11.11) splits from his 9.58 100m record and a corresponding percentage break down of those times. In addition, slower times in intervals of .5 of a second have been listed along with their respective percentage break downs. The shaded areas represent the velocity range between 6 and 8m/s as that zone represents the corporate average velocities that are achieved in the bulk of high intensity running and sprint efforts found in male field sports such as Rugby (League, Union, Sevens), Australian Rules Football, football (soccer), field hockey, Gaelic football, and others.

v30m	95%	90%	85%	80%	75%	70%	65%	60%
11.11	10.55	10.00	9.44	8.89	8.33	7.78	7.22	6.67
10.5	9.98	9.45	8.93	8.40	7.88	7.35	6.83	6.30
10	9.50	9.00	8.50	8.00	7.50	7.00	6.50	6.00
9.5	9.03	8.55	8.08	7.60	7.13	6.65	6.18	5.70
9	8.55	8.10	7.65	7.20	6.75	6.30	5.85	5.40
8.5	8.08	7.65	7.23	6.80	6.38	5.95	5.53	5.10
8	7.60	7.20	6.80	6.40	6.00	5.60	5.20	4.80

v20m	95%	90%	85%	80%	75%	70%	65%	60%
10.1	9.60	9.09	8.59	8.08	7.58	7.07	6.57	6.06
9.5	9.03	8.55	8.08	7.60	7.13	6.65	6.18	5.70
9	8.55	8.10	7.65	7.20	6.75	6.30	5.85	5.40
8.5	8.08	7.65	7.23	6.80	6.38	5.95	5.53	5.10
8	7.60	7.20	6.80	6.40	6.00	5.60	5.20	4.80
7.5	7.13	6.75	6.38	6.00	5.63	5.25	4.88	4.50
7	6.65	6.30	5.95	5.60	5.25	4.90	4.55	4.20
6.5	6.18	5.85	5.53	5.20	4.88	4.55	4.23	3.90

If, for example, we know that the bulk of faster running in these team based field sports is occurring between 6-8 meters per second then the matter of key significance is the maximum of each athlete's speed. The greater the differential between the maximum of speed and the sub-maximal/operational value at which it must be repeated- the greater the speed reserve.

In reference to the chart above we see that the 6-8m/s range represents 60-70% of Bolt's speed over 30m and 60-75% over 20m. Practically speaking, due to the vastly sub-maximal value of this range relative to Bolt's max V, the bulk of the running in most field sports would feel like a routine extensive tempo sessions to him.

Alternatively, for a slower athlete, whose max velocity is 8m/s and 9m/s at 20 and 30m respectively, we see that the shaded areas represent 75-95% and 70-85% of his/her max velocity at each distance. Thus, what for Bolt amounts to an aerobic day at the park is something else entirely for the slower athlete who is faced with a hefty lactic workload.

Couple properly dosed aerobic interval work, such as extensive tempo and not maximal aerobic speed intervals, with pure alactic speed work and the running demands of the majority of team based field sports are covered chapter and verse.

XII. THE DYNAMIC STEREOTYPE

There are important components of adaptation to consider in sport; particularly regarding sports whose primary movement dynamics are rooted in high force: velocity manoeuvres such as sprinting, throwing an implement, swinging an implement, explosive jumps, and more.

Adaptation is, in the most simple terms, a biological self-protection mechanism. It characterizes the defence reactions that are initiated by the organism's complex biological network in response to the various stresses that are incurred in life.

Adaptation in sport is manifested as an increase in any biomotor, biodynamic, or bioenergetic variable. Ideally, the adaptations are relevant with respect to the specifics of the competition structure.

Regarding neuromuscular intensive training, the repetitive exposure to the same/unchanging CNS intensive stimuli presents the possibility of a halt in the adaptation process. This is known as the dynamic stereotype. In this way, the organism stereotypes the training stress that is being ineffectively repetitively exposed and ceases to generate a defence reaction robust enough to yield a performance increase.

While this circumstance may be observed in any number of training scenarios, in sprint development the dynamic stereotype is specific to the repetitive exposure to the same sprint load parameters.

Training variation is essential towards ensuring continued results; however, in sprint development the means by which variety is introduced must be strategically regulated.

XIII. SPRINT TRAINING INTEGRATED INTO THE TRAINING LOAD VIA THE HIGH/LOW METHOD

The High/Low method of training was popularized by no one more so than the late Charlie Francis. It characterizes the organization of training load elements according to their CNS intensiveness in order to optimize workload vs recovery. In this way, all medium or high intensity training elements are consolidated to the same training day and these days are placed adjacent to one or more low intensity training days.

The genius of this system lies in its applicability to multi-targeted sports, in which a variety of biomotor tasks are central to sport performance, and that it allows a greater sum total of high intensity training sessions to be performed over the long term. For example:

- A three high intensity day training week in a high/low scheme might include a Tue/Thu/Sa high intensity schedule in which Mon/Wed/Fri were of low intensity character. In this way, the loading may be carried out for a number of weeks prior to a load reduction becoming necessary. This is because for every high intensity training session, there is a low intensity session, or off day, on either side.

The counter argument to this might suggest that even more high intensity training days be included in a calendar week by varying the means by which movement is executed from day to day. The problem with this, despite the commonality of it, is that the autonomic system, regarding only one biological system, does not care about the kinematics. Thus, even if, in the unlikely event, structural pathologies do not arise as a result of the cumulative loading on consecutive days, the autonomic stress is likely to manifest itself in any number of ways:

- poor sleep quality
- erratic bodyweight fluctuations
- loss of appetite
- general fatigue
- susceptibility to infection/immune suppression

- performance decrease/coordination disruption

Another interesting, and valuable, benefit of the high/low framework is that it allows for a greater sustainability of intensive loading over the long term. Recovery is built into the system and the delicate balance between workload and recovery is preserved. This provides for a greater number of high quality/high intensity sessions to be performed month after month. Thus, regardless if the sport is T&F or any number of multi-targeted disciplines, the high/low split provides for more high intensity training and, by association, the special work capacity (acclimation to high intensity exposure) is enhanced for speed/power disciplines.

Multi-targeted sports must not be limited to team and combat sports. The 100 and 200m sprints in T&F, as two examples of cyclic disciplines, are, in fact, multi-targeted in the biomotor and physiological sense. This is so because of the spectrum of biomotor and physiological qualities that are specific to the high level execution of either of those race distances.

As the number of biodynamic, biomotor, and bioenergetic sport demands begins to rise, so does the suitability of a programming and organizational model that is designed to handle such demands.

A deconstruction of the sport in question is mandatory in order to subdivide and categorize it's kinematic, neuromuscular, and energetic constituents into an appropriate programming and organizational model of preparation. In this way, it is critical to assume a global perspective in order that the deconstruction of the sport includes every aspect of its execution.

A Block Training model, for example, is not suitable for multi-targeted sports because the training load concentration that is essential to the Block Method is not appropriate to direct towards more than a few targets.

A vertically integrated model (originally popularized by the late Charlie Francis), which is a concurrent or complex-parallel system, provides for a multitude of biodynamic, biomotor, bioenergetic training components to exist and develop simultaneously via the strategic manipulation of the proportionality that exists between the various load elements.

The development of sprint speed, regardless of whether the athlete is a T&F sprinter, jumper, field, or court sport athlete, includes a mosaic of biomotor necessities. Consider Kurt Meinel's Motor Quality Framework as shared by French T&F Coach Pierre Jean Vazel in a Q&A with Jimson Lee on www.speedendurance.com: **the fundamental structure of movement is made of the specific rhythm and coupling of fluidity, precision, consistency, intensity, speed and amplitude.**

These six motor qualities constitute the basal movement elements of nearly all sport manoeuvres rooted in reactive/elastic and explosive tasks. Any coach or sport enthusiast that observes an athlete execute sport manoeuvres and states "*now that is a great athlete*" is effectively stating "*look at that individual's specific rhythm and coupling of fluidity, precision, consistency, intensity, speed, and amplitude*". As to how these qualities may be developed in an athlete, aside from what is already intrinsic relative to genetically passed on material, the solution lies in the loading; how to manage the workload versus recovery. Such is the foundation of the high/low framework.

In a high/low system, all training components that register medium to high in neuromuscular intensity are consolidated to the same day. The reason for consolidating the medium intensity work, specifically if it presents structural stress to the same body segments that are central to the highest intensity training elements, to the high intensity days is because the medium intensity zone is just stressful enough to prohibit full recovery within a 24 hour period yet it is just weak enough, on its own, to prohibit performance enhancement in a variety of speed/power contexts.

The instance in which all CNS intensive loading would not be consolidated to the same training day is during a general physical preparation (GPP) stage; regardless of sport. A properly structured GPP period does include any training components of particularly high neuromuscular stress and thus the workload may be distributed over a greater number of training opportunities/days. This is analogous to generating a greater surface area over which force is sustained and incrementally reducing the surface area, over time, in order to generate a greater stimulus to the designated area(s).

Two training week examples for a sprinter are illustrated below. The first one representative of a week during the GPP period and the second during the special physical preparation (SPP) period. In both cases, the integrity of the high/low framework is preserved within a vertically integrated structure.

GPP

Monday	Tuesday	Wednesday	Thursday	Friday	Saturday
MB Throws	Hill Sprints	MB Throws	Hill Sprints	MB Throws	Hill Sprints
Upper body wts	Jumps	Upper body wts	Jumps	Upper body wts	Jumps
Tempo	Lower wts	Tempo	Lower wts	Tempo	Lower wts

SPP

Monday	Tuesday	Wednesday	Thursday	Friday	Saturday
Auxiliary wts	Acceleration emphasis	Auxiliary wts	Special End Emphasis	Auxiliary wts	Max Velocity Emphasis
Tempo		Tempo		Tempo	
	Explosive Throws		Explosive Throws		Explosive Throws
	Explosive Jumps		Explosive Jumps		Explosive Jumps
	Total Primary wts		Total Primary wts		Total Primary wts

More comprehensive training load examples, taken from actual programs created for various speed/power athletes, are provided at the end of this manual. The program excerpts feature means by which sprint training is integrated into the training load via the high/low framework.

Anaerobic-lactic runs must be accounted for as high intensity in a high/low system. Important to point out, however, is the velocity associated with the runs. As previously discussed, MAS, 300yd shuttle, and Yo-Yo protocols are characterized by relatively slow/low velocity running. The reason the bioenergetic stress is lactic is due to either the incomplete recoveries or sustained efforts. In the high/low framework any anaerobic-lactic runs must be placed on a high intensity day which means they must either replace or follow a vital speed oriented session.

While the development of sprint speed is central to so many sports, it must be accompanied by the development of all other required skills that, together, prepare the athlete for the competitive demands. The identification of the specific training components that must be addressed, for any particular sport, are the product of the process of deconstruction that is initiated from a global perspective. The process of identifying the basal constituents of sprinting is no different and it begins with assuming a global perspective over the applied sciences that relate to the sprint action.

XIV. APPLIED SCIENCES

The next series of sections represent subjective viewpoints on the practical applications and considerations of physics, biomechanics, and physiology. Any coach of any sport is well served to strive towards being an applied physicist/biomechanist/physiologist as well as psychologist. As the complete, and theoretical, mastery of this objective is arguably the sum of many lifetimes of work, there is certainly no justification for any coach in the world slowing in their quest for knowledge in these domains.

XIV.1. APPLIED PHYSICS

Newton's laws of motion reveal a great deal about the physics of sprinting. Here, only the broad strokes will be discussed for practical purposes.

Newton's 1st Law- *An object at rest stays at rest and an object in motion stays in motion with the same speed and in the same direction unless acted upon by an unbalanced force.*

The practical points to consider here regard initiating a sprint from a static start, redirecting a sprint into a vector different from the initial one (displacement), decelerating or stopping a sprint, accelerating and, regarding team and combat sport athletes, the nature of encountering an unbalanced force .

XIV.1.1. INITIATING A SPRINT FROM A STATIC START

An athlete at rest prior to initiating a sprint effort must deal with overcoming their own static inertia. The question then becomes what is the athletes bodymass as that is the first problem to solve regarding the forces he/she must generate in order to maximize their starting ability. In his texts Special Strength Training and Super Training, the late Dr. Yuri Verkhoshansky elaborated upon starting strength as the ability to generate force at the beginning of muscle contraction. It occurs prior to external movement and it is represented as the line tangent to the force: time curve. In this way, it is graphically similar to the slope of sprint acceleration that is much steeper prior to reaching the 30m mark . In the case of starting strength, the steeper the slope, or rate, of force increase the better.

Starting strength is not to be confused in any way with maximal strength as the latter is representative of the maximum of force generation irrespective of time. As one might think, methods of developing starting strength are specific to exerting explosive force, against sub-maximal external loading or bodyweight, from a static position- none more specific than practicing the starting position as it relates to the competitive requirements.

The greater the athlete's bodymass the greater the impulse and accelerative forces required to start and accelerate. By association, acceleration strength characterizes the time signature of maximal force development prior to and once external movement occurs. In this way, it follows starting strength on the time line (comes second in the order of events).

A point worth clarifying is that athletes of larger bodymass do not necessarily need to be absolutely or relatively strong in order to be explosive starters. This may seem counterintuitive; however, in the context of a sprint start, starting and acceleration strength are entirely a function of time; whereas maximal strength is not. For this reason, defensive tackles in American football, for example, who easily average in excess of 135kg/297lbs and explosive take-off ability is central to their positional requirements, do not have to be particularly maximally strong in hip/leg exercise such as a squat- to have explosive take-off ability. The reason is because the inertia they must overcome is equal to their bodymass and the prospect of defensive tackle being able to explosively negotiate a load, via a hip/leg dominant action, as small as their own bodymass is a foregone conclusion.

Practical Example:
- *In 2009 I prepared a defensive tackle for an NFL pro day. At that time he weighed approximately 135kg/298lb. At his NFL pro day he ran, hand timed so that must be taken for what it's worth, the 40yd (36.576m) in 4.85-4.92seconds (depending on which evaluator I talked to), vertically leaped 31.5in/80cm, and broad jumped 9'3"/2.82m. All decent numbers for American footballer of that bodymass, particularly his superb power index (square root of bodymass multiplied by square root of VJ in imperial values); however, from a maximal strength perspective he was challenged to squat much more than 500lbs/~227kg. While the 500lbs was an unimpressive number for a man of that size to squat it was still 200lbs in excess of his bodymass. This combined with his intrinsic reactive/elastic qualities and effective training proved sufficient for him to score strong marks in the speed/explosive strength evaluations which, in practical terms, contributed to him possessing superb take-off ability for a man that size.*

31.5"/80cm Vertical Jump at 298lb/135kg

Alternatively, once the American football down linemen make contact with their opponent a new argument presents itself which, unlike the previous example, is heavily weighted in the value of maximal strength qualities. This will be left reserved for the discussion regarding an athlete encountering an unbalanced force.

XIV.1.2. DISPLACING A FORCE VECTOR AND DECELERATION

A vector has both magnitude and direction. The magnitude being related to the propulsive forces associated with the movement. Thus, the greater the rate of change in velocity, bodymass, in addition to the greater the degree of direction change, the greater the forces required for displacing the original force vector.

There are a multitude of forces contributing to the net force total during the displacement (vertical, braking, applied...). The applied biomechanics section will address the movement qualities necessary to optimize this task. Here we will discuss the physics applications.

From Fnet = mass x acceleration we know that a heavier athlete moving at an acceleration X has bigger problems to solve than a small athlete moving at the same acceleration when it comes time to rapidly change direction or decelerate in the same line of travel. It is mandatory that the athletes decelerate in both cases; however, the degree of deceleration required is relative to the forces the athletes are able to apply specific to each action.

- A note on deceleration- in physics, any change in velocity is an acceleration. The slowing of speed is a change in velocity. Thus, while the common speak refers to a decrease in speed as deceleration, in physics terms both the increase as well as decrease in speed is termed acceleration due to the change in velocity. For our purposes here, however, a decrease in speed will be termed a deceleration.

The ground contact times associated with either changing direction or decelerating will always be longer then the ground contact times associated with accelerating in a linear path. For this reason, relative strength qualities play a more profound role in change of direction work and decelerating in comparison to accelerating up to and including maximum velocity and beyond; in which reactive/elastic qualities prevail.

As both change of direction and deceleration actions are time specific in sport, however, the time dependent qualities of force production remain at the forefront of athlete preparation.

One need not consider the nature of this discussion to polarize the significance of various forms of training, however. It is not a question of placing velocity based training against slow strength training. The key is to understand, similar to the strategic implications of long to short, combined, and short to long on all sports training, the proportionality and contribution of the various motor qualities to the various sprint/acceleration/deceleration related efforts.

Further, it is necessary to weigh these considerations against the particulars of the athletes.

Regarding the context of developing sprint speed, it is reasonable to state that every sprint athlete's output capabilities represent one of three biomotor domains: from left to right on the F(t) curve
- Reactive/Elastic
- Combined
- Strength

Those who have been coaching long enough will recognize that some of their fastest athletes were:
- incredibly reactive/elastic, very light on their feet, short amplitude and rapid countermovements on jumping exercises, quick ground contacts when bounding, though not particularly impressive in the weight room
- very strong in the weight room, longer amplitude countermovements on jumping exercises, longer ground contact times on multi-response jumps
- or a combination of the two

This reality indicates that the variability in motor qualities possessed by both pure sprinters as well as any 'fast' athlete similarly demands variability in coaching methodics that suit these different populations. For this reason, some of the most talented sprinters in T&F history executed completely different types of training plans.

For example, Carl Lewis did not train with weights, at all, until the last year of his career (which at that time was past his greatest accomplishments). Alternatively, Ben Johnson possessed weight room abilities that rival any world class powerlifter.

Carl performed a great deal of jumping and bounding exercises in his program; reflective of the fact that he, in his words, was a long jumper who sprinted. Additionally, we must acknowledge the fact that his coach, Tom Tellez (who Dan Pfaff described to me during a private conversation as the most profound applied biomechanist he has ever encountered) was clearly playing towards Carl's strengths as a reactive/elastic dominant motor type.

Alternatively, in Ben Johnson's case, whom his coach Charlie Francis described as having suffered from chondromalacia patella, did not perform any jumping exercises in his training; though his fantastic strength resulted in him bench pressing over 200kg x 1 and squatting 600lb x 6 at a bodyweight of less than 80kg.

What's more, it is necessary to point out that training with weights is in no way the only means of strength training; or assessment. In fact, as in any physical endeavour, leverages are central to performance. For this reason, it is irresponsible to measure an athlete's specific force output via an exercise that does not closely approximate their competition manoeuvres and accommodate their anthropometry.

Ultimately, a measure of specific maximal force is ideally reserved for the competition manoeuvre itself (which requires sophisticated diagnostic equipment short of the athlete competing in a barbell sport) or the closest dynamic approximation (which, depending upon the movement, may prove much more feasible). In contrast, more often in sport preparation, an athletes maximal force ability is irresponsibly measured via movements that are non-specific in relation to the biomechanics of their sport requirements. In this way, the coaching staff runs the risk of validating many false positives as improvements in general strength certainly serve a purpose, up to a point; however, as sport mastery improves any improvements in general strength become less significant.

There are optimal anthropometric proportions for any physical action. Consider Usain Bolt and Randy Barnes, the world record holders in the 100m/200m and Indoor/Outdoor Shot Put, respectively. Regarding only physical attributes, it is plain to state that each man possesses visually observable physical features that lend themselves towards each man excelling in their respective disciplines. Similarly, so do many of their competitors; even if they, at first, appear to be built quite differently. It's a matter of proportions.

We know that the fastest sprinters, regardless of their bodymass or height, all share similar proportions in terms of the ratios between torso length (shorter) to leg length (longer), small waists, etcetera. We also know that long levers are similarly valuable, and shared in common, with elite shot put athletes; only the throwers possess much greater bodymass and girth dimensions in order to generate the forces specific to throwing the 7.26kg shot as far as possible.

Thus, while the fastest sprinters and the farthest throwers each, respectively, share anthropometric proportions in common with their peers, no sprinter or thrower would think to compete in the others competitive domain.

In any case, regarding the highest level performers, there are far greater anthropometric proportional similarities, shared between competitors of the same discipline, than there are differences.

XIV.13. ACCELERATION

Once the inertia is overcome at the start, more and more force must be applied into the ground in order to accelerate with every step. Otherwise, the state of motion achieved as a result of the starting effort would remain unchanged. Thus, momentum (mass x velocity) is generated with every step- provided the force applied into the ground increases with every step- as it does up until maximum velocity is attained.

While different facets of resistance training may certainly supplement a sprint program, there is no effective replacement for sprint training itself- only alternatives in cases of environmental or facility restrictions or injury.

A point of interest regarding the polarity of propulsive mechanisms associated with the start, acceleration and maximum velocity: The closer to the point of overcoming static inertia (the start) the more the propulsive machinery is rooted in muscle/mechanical energy. Then, as momentum builds and the athletes approaches and reaches maximum velocity, the predominance of propulsive mechanisms shifts to reflexive/reactive/elastic qualities.

Subjectively, the feeling of the start and early acceleration is pronounced in terms of the physical effort/energy required to get going. As the athlete assumes the upright (sprint) position and approaches maximum velocity the sensation then shifts to near weightlessness such that the 'feeling' of effort/energy during the start and early acceleration is vastly diminished. Some sprinters actually describe difficulty in feeling their legs much at all once they are at maximum velocity. Another factor that reinforces the relaxation and lack of 'trying to sprint as fast as possible' associated with the fastest sprinters.

XIV.1.4. AN ATHLETE ENCOUNTERING AN UNBALANCED FORCE

While time dependent strength qualities are essential for speed related objectives, a different problem presents itself when an athlete is acted upon by an unbalanced force such as an implement or opponent.

The greater the mass of the sport implement and the greater the force: velocity characteristics presented by an opponent- the greater the demand for maximal strength qualities from the athlete. In this way, the difference in bodymass and force outputs between javelin throwers and shot put athletes corresponds to the mass of the respective implements. In both cases, however, the speed of force production is central to the competition outcome.

In the case of team and combat sports, the nature of the competitive requirements assumes a greater degree of complexity due to the dynamics of reacting to another dynamic system- the opponent. Take American football down linemen, for example: over time the positional requirements have mandated that athletes bodymass remain consistent with what is necessary to both withstand as well as overcome each positional opponent's bodymass and force: velocity outputs. Offensive and defensive linemen carry the greatest bodymass indexes on the field and thus while time dependent force qualities are essential for speed related objective, time independent force qualities are essential once contact is made with the opposing and unbalanced force presented by the opponent.

Non-time dependent force potential is correlated to cross-sectional diameter of muscle fibre. This is why, the athletes who possess the greatest degrees of maximal strength are also the athletes who possess greater amounts of bodymass. Athletes who are faced with the challenge of sustaining as well as overcoming opponents who possess great bodymass as well as force: velocity outputs must, therefore, not limit their positional requirements to acceleration based development alone.

Newton's 2nd Law- *commonly recognized as force = mass x acceleration may also be illustrated as acceleration = force(net)/mass. In any case, the acceleration is proportional to the magnitude of net force, and in the same direction, and inversely proportional to the mass. Therefore it is more accurate to illustrate the common equation as f(net) = m x a*

The practical considerations here, the context being directed towards acceleration development, are rooted in the following:

- acceleration is the multiplier (hence "speed kills")
- net force being unchanged, the lesser the mass the greater the acceleration
- mass being unchanged, acceleration is dependent upon increased net force application

It is useful to identify the types of forces:

- frictional
- tension
- normal
- air resistance
- applied
- spring
- gravitational
- electrical
- magnetic

While nearly every type of force is pertinent to sprinting, we will only concern ourselves here with the discussion of practically applied concepts regarding the forces generated by the athlete.

XIV.1.5. SPEED KILLS

Regarding net force production, acceleration is the multiplier and thus its impact cannot be underestimated. The discussion of force, in this context, is incomplete without elaborating upon all of the forces (hence net force) acting on an object. Air resistance, gravitational pull, and friction are just a few of the factors affecting the sprint action. Most important, we must recognize the value of time dependent athlete generated force qualities being more relevant for sprint/acceleration development.

For example, an uninformed coach might mistakenly assume that more force, void of specification, at a given bodymass will enhance acceleration ability. This would result in the idea that simply getting an athlete stronger (maximally for example), provided bodymass is held constant, will result in greater acceleration ability. This is an incomplete notion. We must account for the fact that time is of the essence. Otherwise, the preparation of an athlete for the sole purpose of acceleration development may be limited to increasing the maximal force capability of the athlete and holding their bodymass constant. If only it were so easy...

The training problem of acceleration development is a variable one as the dynamics change with every step. As speed increases more force is generated at ground contact; however, as the speed increases there is less time to apply force.

During early acceleration, the ground contact times (GCT) are longer (because the acceleration is slower) and longer GCT provides more time to apply force. This is more forgiving for an athlete who, regardless of bodymass, is capable of generating high levels of explosive force. This is why an explosive athlete of greater bodymass (such as a shot putter or heavyweight Olympic weightlifter) can execute impressive sprint times over very short distances. Note that it is not the force production alone that is relevant here, but the rate at which these athletes are able to apply great forces.

Alternatively, as the acceleration increases, and GCT becomes shorter, the athlete has less time to apply force. Now the circumstances favour those with greater reactive/elastic qualities as the environment demands that more and more net force be applied to overcome the mass and as speed increases it becomes less and less possible for muscle/mechanical work to get the job done.

At this point is noteworthy to point out that there is a continuum of propulsive machinery; not harsh lines that divide the contributions of muscle/mechanical and reactive/elastic work. In this way, the discussion is similar to what will be presented in the applied physiology section regarding how there are distinct bioenergetic fuel sources; however, at no single time is any one bioenergetic fuel source responsible for muscle contraction.

World class biomechanists and coaches, such as Frans Bosch and Dan Pfaff, have elaborated upon the fact that reactive/elastic qualities are present from the very beginning of a sprint because even during early acceleration the sprinter demonstrates observable oscillations; and if oscillations are present so are reactive/elastic contributions. By contrast, there are no observable movement oscillations demonstrated during a tonic strength exercise such as a heavy deadlift; and thus the development of reactive/elastic qualities are not relevant towards improving a limit deadlift result.

XIV.1.6. NET FORCE BEING CONSTANT, THE LESSER THE MASS THE GREATER THE ACCELERATION

It is for this reason why two automobiles may move at entirely different rates of acceleration if the only difference between them is that one of them is of considerably less mass than the other. The reduction of mass is not always beneficial in sport, however. Certain sport disciplines/positional requirements present disadvantageous circumstances for an athlete who is of insufficient bodymass (such as Rugby front row forwards, American football down linemen, and weight class division combat and strength athletes). In all cases, as previously discussed, an athletes reduction in bodymass ceases to be an advantage when their ability to sustain the unbalanced force of their opponents (or sport implement) becomes compromised- an ability that is dependent upon more than force production alone.

XIV.1.7. MASS BEING CONSTANT, ACCELERATION IS DEPENDENT UPON INCREASED NET FORCE APPLICATION

Again, 'net' being the operative word because, as it pertains to this discussion, the specific nature of force that is applied has tremendous implications of the movement outcome. In coaching circles, experience has shown that it always proves useful to use the simplest analogies; such as those that regard lifting weights.

Imagine that the concept of time dependent force being applied to a deadlift competition. In this way, the contest result would not hinge on the amount of weight that is lifted. The load, or mass, in fact, would remain constant. The competition would be who could lift the barbell to lockout with the greatest speed. The question then becomes, how much weight is on the bar (what is its mass); as the mass has profound effects, as previously discussed, on the net force requirement relative to acceleration.

Vladimir Zatsiorsky explained how maximal strength ceases to have an effect on endurance qualities once the load that must be overcome descends beneath 30% of the maximum of achievable force. The development of speed qualities isn't much different. This is why the sprinter who can squat, or leg press, or split squat, or lunge... the most weight, in no way provides any indication that he/she is the fastest sprinter.

In the deadlift for speed competition then, if the bar weight was such that it was well beneath even the sub-maximal realm of each athletes strength ability, such as an empty 20kg barbell alone, then the determining factor would not be the athletes maximal strength.

In Zatsiorsky's "Science and Practice of Strength Training" he describes the Explosive Strength Deficit as the difference between the maximum force an athlete can generate in a given unit of time and the maximum force the athlete can generate under the most beneficial conditions (no time limit). Zatsiorsky states that the ESD represents the percentage of the athlete's strength potential that is not used in a given attempt.

In maximum velocity sprinting, the world's elite may generate a "peak" force up to 5 times their own bodyweight at ground contact in less then a tenth of a second. Consider an 85kg (185lb) sprinter moving at 12m/s in which case it is reasonable to consider a peak force during ground contact (less than .1 of a second) that may reach 425kg (935lb). There is no weight training action that can approach this sort of force generation in that amount of time. This diminishes the correlation between maximal strength and maximum velocity as the former exists independent of time and the latter lives and dies by it.

Alternatively, during the start and acceleration the velocity is less and therefore, as previously discussed, the significance of maximal strength, particularly the strength as it relates to the bodymass, plays a greater role in overcoming static inertia and early acceleration. To reiterate, non-time dependent strength qualities (ergo maximal strength) are more relevant the slower the movement and time dependent strength qualities (ergo speed strength) are more relevant the faster the movement.

Newton's 3rd Law- *For every action there is an equal and opposite reaction*

In sprinting, there is more than one force vector being generated by the sprinter. A horizontal as well as a vertical one. Here is it useful to discuss the concept of negative foot speed.

The sprinter builds speed as a result of delivering greater and greater forces into the ground with each step (up to maximum velocity). The key to generating greater force with each step is associated with cycling the recovery leg in such a way that as the foot approaches the ground it is moving backwards at a faster rate then the ground is moving underneath the sprinter. This is negative foot speed. This is simpler than it sounds.

- Think of a bicycle turned upside down. You begin slapping a tire to get the wheel to spin. In order to increase the rotational speed of the wheel you must swing your arm/hand faster, and in the same direction, then the rotational velocity of the wheel with each slap.

The paradox of increasing sprint speed and ground contact (peak) force may be framed as the following duality:

- Increased time dependent ground contact force provides for increased sprint speed
- Increased sprint speed generates increased time dependent ground contact force

Considering how slightly built sprinters are capable of generating +11m/s it is logical to suggest that volitional muscle/mechanically generated ground impact forces front load the start and early acceleration and as speed increases the sprinter's volitional force generating efforts diminish in favour of frequency based reactive/elastic efforts in which the increased ground impact forces are a bi-product.

The irony then becomes that as the sprinter builds speed the less they are making a volitional effort to generate more force; even though more and more force is generated at greater speeds. In this way, a curious "chicken and egg" relationship exists between speed and force; though it is viable to suggest that force follows speed- and so do weights.

XIV.18. WEIGHTS FOLLOW SPEED

This was first established by the late Charlie Francis. It is noteworthy to mention Charlie's findings: Ben Johnson worked up to a bench press single of nearly 202kg/~444.4lb for one repetition the week prior to the 100m final in the 1988 Olympics in Seoul. Charlie stated this happened by mistake due to an error in accounting for the fact that the bumper plates were calibrated in kilos as opposed to imperial pounds. Thus, what was intended to be 365lb/~165.9kg on the bar for a sub-maximal final strength stimulus resulted in 202kg. Charlie also stated that the loading of the bench press in Ben's program leading up to that point in no way suggested that he was capable of lifting 202kg. The question then becomes how was it possible for Ben Johnson, at 173lb/~78.63kg bodyweight, to lift such an impressive weight in the bench press.

A first hand account of the same phenomenon:

- *In the summer of 2010 while coaching at the University level I devised a special program for the starting running back (currently on injured reserve in the NFL). He had undergone surgery to repair a damaged ligament in his wrist and as a result he could not load his wrist for a period of 8 weeks. During that time I assembled a modified training regimen for him that worked around the structural limitations of his wrist yet still allowed him to make linear improvements in his speed, reactive/elastic, explosive, and force dominant abilities specific to his legs and hips and , impressively, sustain minimal losses in upper body strength (a credit to general organism strength).*

- *He was only limited in his ability to load his wrist. All upper body training was relegated to the sub-maximal and auxiliary domain and mandated that all external loads were secured to his*

forearm with velcro straps and belts; proximal to the affected area of his wrist. In this way, he was able to perform various rows, shoulder and arm exercises, shrugs, and chest fly motion; in addition to his routine neck exercises. During these 8 weeks he was unable to perform any movements that loaded his wrist; no exercises that place an external load in his hand.

- *While a certain volume of his upper body training regimen included single arm sub-maximal muscle lengthening movements, for the unaffected limb (for the cross-over effect), this volume of training was relatively insignificant relative to the complex of all other elements.*

- *Regarding the lower body training he was unaffected and thus participated in the training with the rest of his position group. This included alactic linear and multi-directional sprint work, reactive/elastic and explosive jumps, and lower body non-time dependent force training which for him predominantly included squats with the safety-squat bar, leg presses, and back raises.*

- *In using a modified version of Charlie's GPP in which speed work progresses from hills to the flats and weights undergo an accumulation followed by a 3-1-3 seven week intensification scheme he eventually worked up to a 535lb/~243kg squat with the safety bar at 185lb/~84kg bodyweight. Not only was that lift impressive on it's own; particularly relative to his*  *bodyweight, but even more so considering the fact that he had not once squatted a weight much in excess of 300lbs since he underwent the repair to his wrist.*

- *What I had told him was that the squat exercise was serving as his primary general organism strength stimulus (as far as the weight training was concerned) until he could load his upper body more aggressively; and that if he felt good on any given day then he should exploit that feeling of readiness.*

- *During the accumulation stage I did not assign specific loads for his squat work. We followed a plan similar to Charlie's in which all speed work (jumps and so on) was completed prior to heading to the weight room. By the time we got to the weight room I told him just to go by feel. Throughout the entire accumulation phase, and up to the point during max strength, he used sub-maximal loads for all squat sessions; most often ranging from 250-300lbs. Then during one particular session during max strength, when the other players were lifting in sets of 3-5 reps, he felt like working up to a single. The end result was 535lbs.*

- *Anyone reviewing his training plan during that time would be challenged to determine how it* *was possible for him to squat that amount of weight if their review was **limited his squat work alone.***

In both the running back's as well as Ben Johnson's case, the reason for the impressive weights lifted can in no way be attributed solely to the weight training. Herein lies the implication of the speed work and the nature of load in general.

Addition, as one of the most basic tenets of arithmetic, provides a great deal of information regarding the nature of load; in so far as all loads are cumulative.

Consider the following categories of training elements and the arbitrary values that have been assigned to them respective to neuromuscular demand (influenced by Charlie Francis' Motor Unit Recruitment Chart):

Category 1- Value of 5
  • Alactic Speed work, Maximal Intensity Olympic Weightlifts, Shock Training, Explosive Throws
Category 2- Value of 4
  • Speed Endurance, Maximal intensity squats and deadlifts
Category 3- Value of 3
  • Special Endurance, Maximal intensity bench press
Category 4- Value of 2
  • Tempo Runs, Middle and Long distance runs, Maximal intensity arm pulling exercises
Category 5- Value of 1
  • Auxiliary weight training, jogging

From this example we may conclude that the addition of three training elements each from category 1 and 2 results in greater sum totals then the addition of three training elements each from categories 4 and 5.

The greater the neuromuscular value of the training the greater the neuromuscular stimulus; and thus the greater the load intensity.

In both Ben Johnson's and the running back's case, the factor that must be counted towards the impressive weights lifted is the contribution of the speed work towards the cumulative total. Clearly in Ben's case this contribution was gigantic as reflected by his sprint speed. Never the less, in the running back's case, not only was he performing acceleration based alactic sprint work, he was also performing explosive jumps. Both training elements that exist in the higher categories of neuromuscular stress and, therefore, valuable factors that contribute to higher general organism strength in the spirit of getting 'strong' anywhere improves 'strength' everywhere.

Further, within 10 days of the running back's wrist brace being removed he bench pressed in excess of 90% of his previous maximum- having not touched a barbell in 8 weeks. His previous max in the bench press was 355lbs (161kg). His 10th day after being able to load his wrist he bench pressed 330lbs (150kg) with his feet up on the bench (no leg drive). This further validates the principle of general organism strength due to the contribution of the sprint, jump, as well as squat work. Had his leg/hip strength not possessed the potential to squat in excess of 230kg, had his acceleration ability not been pronounced, and had he not already been very strong prior to becoming injured, there would be no way to explain the weights he lifted; particularly in the post injury bench press as he had not loaded that movement in more than 2 months.

General organism strength characterizes the implications of neuromuscular advancements in one region of the body on any other region of the body as all peripheral actions are mobilized by the same central machinery. The significance of this lies in the logic of maximizing biomotor outputs all over the body, regardless of sport requirements while remaining within bodymass requirements. Should an athlete sustain an injury to any limb the degree to which they will be able to generate a general organism stimulus hinges entirely on their ability to generate high outputs via the unaffected limbs of the body. Thus, for example: any speed/power athlete who sustains a leg injury, regardless of the direct contribution of upper body strength to the competition exercise, will be limited in stimulating the affected limb(s) during their road to return based upon their ability to generate high outputs via their upper body.

XIV.2. APPLIED BIOMECHANICS

This section will address practically applied mechanical principles as they pertain to economizing the movement of the human body; specifically as it relates to sprinting.

XIV.2.1. THE START

In any sports endeavour that involves initiating a sprint from a static start, not limited to T&F, the following question must be answered:

- what is the optimal mechanical position for the athlete to be in in order to overcome their static inertia with the greatest speed

As a result, the next question regards the sport/context/scenario. We will hold fast to the, in the words of Dan Pfaff, 'biomechanical truths' that serve to unify various movement forms. Biomechanical truths characterize movement efficiencies which transcend athlete specifics and are, thus, aspects of training that coaches and athletes must universally strive towards.

In any land based sport in which an athlete is initiating a sprint from a static start, the athlete can only be in one of 4 primary orientations:

- In full contact with the ground (prone, supine, or side lying)
- In 2 points of contact with the ground (any variety of a standing or kneeling starts)
- In 3 points of contact with the ground (a low start with one hand down in support along with both feet)
- In 4 points of contact with the ground (a low start such as a block start in T&F or a 4pt stance that an American football defensive tackle might use in which both hands are down in support along with both feet)

Far too often, regarding non-track sports, athletes are tasked with executing sprints from these various start positions void of the proper mechanical instruction of how to get out that particular position in the first place. Executing these various starting positions with efficiency/the least amount of wasted movement, requires as much attention to biomechanical detail as the acceleration mechanics themselves.

XIV.2.2. STARTING FROM THE PRONE, SUPINE, OR SIDE LYING POSITION

In field and court based sports, for example, there are instances in which an athlete may find themselves having to initiate a sprint/acceleration from the prone, supine, or side lying position on the ground.

In any case, the objective is for the athlete to reposition him/herself for the optimal takeoff into bipedal acceleration. In all cases, prone/supine/side lying, the objective is to attain a low starting position in the shortest amount of time as a lower centre of mass is more advantage for overcoming static inertia in a horizontal direction.

XIV.2.2.B. THE PRONE POSITION

The face forward prone start position requires that the athlete execute an explosive pushup in order to provide the space necessary to thrust the lead knee forward which allows for the ground contact of the lead leg to occur just behind the hips (this is key and will be further discussed in the three and four point start position section). In this way, the athlete will achieve an efficient low start position as they initiate the take-off. The prone position is the most favourable one to be in, relative to supine or side lying, as it is the closest in proximity and requires the least amount of movement to achieve the optimal take-off. The movement sequence described here requires one compound manoeuvre for the athlete to achieve the low start position- explosive pushup while simultaneously thrusting the lead knee forward.

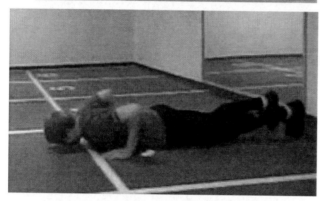

XIV.2.2.C. THE SUPINE POSITION

The supine start position (lying on one's back), in which the athlete's head is facing the same direction as the subsequent sprint, requires that the execute an explosive transition to the 3 or 4 point starting position. This may be accomplished in more than one way. The least time consuming method is to roll into the prone position and then initiate the same movement sequence as when initiating the sprint from the prone position. Thus 2 moves are requires: roll to prone position + explosive pushup while simultaneously thrusting the lead knee forward.

Athletes will often mistakenly attempt to first execute trunk flexion (a sit up) as they begin to transfer/roll/rotate into the 3 or 4 point low start. This, in fact, requires more time as three movements must be made prior to the athlete assuming the low start position. The only instance in which it is mechanically advisable for the athlete to flex their trunk in order to initiate the exit from the supine position is if the direction of the sprint is opposite the direction of their head in the supine position. In this way, the athlete will flex their spine as they pivot on their hip into the face forward prone position. From here they will execute the same movement sequence as the prone start.

XIV.2.2.D. THE SIDE LYING POSITION

The side lying start position, in which the athlete is lying on their left or right side parallel to the long axis of their take-off direction, requires two moves to achieve the optimal start position: Roll to the prone position + Explosive Pushup while simultaneously thrusting the lead knee forward.

In all cases, prone/supine/side lying, the predominance of discussion has been limited to a starting direction in which the athlete has be lying with their head in the same direction as the take-off direction. Clearly, in field/court sports it is equally as common for an athlete to find themselves having to recover from a prone/supine/side lying position in which the direction of their head is not the same as the required take-off direction. In this way, the beginning orientation of the athlete's head may be horizontal, 180 degrees opposite, or any angle in between relative to the optimal take-off direction. In order to optimize mechanical efficiency the athlete must work to minimize the time, resultant of finding the harmony between the number of movements as well as the working effort, required to achieve the optimal start position. This may very well differ from one athlete to the next based upon their anthropometry and explosive output potential to manipulate their own bodymass.

XIV.2.3. 2 POINTS OF CONTACT

XIV.2.3.A. ONE KNEE DOWN

Not only is a one knee down kneeling position useful for training purposes, due to the mechanical overload placed upon the lead leg during take-off, it also is a position many field and court sport athletes may find themselves having to recover from during competition.

In this case, regardless if the athlete is already facing in the same direction of the take-off, the athlete is situated in a starting position and the next move becomes initiating the take-off. It is mandatory that the athlete maintain a line of extension through the lumbar spine and hips such that stiffness is maintained which enhances the force transduction properties of the body compartments through which energy is transmitted from the lead/support leg, drive leg and opposing arm.

The optimal single knee down kneeling start position, provided the athlete is facing in the same direction of the take-off, will have the athletes lead leg knee positioned forward of the ankle. This will provide the positive shin angle that is intrinsic to optimizing initial acceleration as well as the departure angle which corresponds with the position that allows the athlete to

capitalize upon both horizontal and vertical take-off forces. Here, an interesting phenomenon presents itself- the shin angle , in the starting position, of the lead leg in the one leg kneeling as well as 3 and 4pt starts corresponds very closely to the departure angle of extension of the athletes body. This has been observed time and time again in slow motion video analysis of various athletes initiating a sprint out of any of those starting positions. While there is a certain degree of deviation, in terms of the static shin angle relative to the subsequent line of body extension, from athlete to athlete, the commonality cannot be ignored.

In this way, it is optimal for the athlete to position the angle of their torso in such a way that it corresponds to the shin angle of the leg leg. From here, the propulsive forces generated by the arm opposite the trail leg, the push off from the lead leg, and the drive through of the trail leg are what propels the athlete out of the single leg kneeling position. The greater the strength of the lumbar erectors the more able the athlete will be able to maintain extension through the hips as they exit the kneeling position.

XIV.2.3.A. 2 POINTS OF CONTACT- STANDING START POSITION

The two point standing start is the most common starting position for the bulk of athletes including T&F jumpers, the Javelin throw, 800m, middle and long distance runners, field, and court sport athletes.

The kinematics of the starting position will vary from event to event and sport to sport relative to the nature of the task at hand.

Irrespective of the event discipline or sport, if the only goal is to achieve the fastest possible start from the standing position then the athlete must honour certain biomechanical truths. The problem of overcoming static inertia during a sprint start is solved via the athlete achieving a take-off angle that plays towards their output abilities relative to the task of optimizing the application of vertical and horizontal forces. For this reason, the take-off angle will differ from one athlete to the next; and by association so will the kinematics of their starting position.

Of the multitude of biomechanical markers there are to analyse regarding the start, some of the most prominent are the take-off angle, the athletes ability to maintain hip extension, and subsequent shin angle during the first few steps of acceleration.

Regarding the take-off angle, the 45 degree mark has proven itself advantageous over time due to the orientation that allows the athlete to maximize vertical and horizontal force application.

Deviations from this angle must be made relative to the athlete's output ability, however. The key is that the athlete is able to maintain hip extension throughout the take-off and acceleration; as losses in hip extension limit the force application of each stride.

Thus, regardless of the angle of complete extension relative to the ground, the most important factor is that the athlete achieves complete extension. Athletes who possess greater output ability and strength throughout the spinal erectors are able to maintain a more acute angle of complete extension, relative to the ground, during the start and early acceleration. It is these athletes who will typically execute take-offs at an angle closer to the ground- yet still maintain complete extension with every ground contact.

Athletes who are not as powerful will benefit from a greater departure angle at take-off. This is because more output is required to prevent an athlete from falling on their face who is attempting to accelerate at more of an acute angle of extension in relation to the ground. This has implications on the kinematics of both the standing start as well as the 3 and 4 point low starts.

In the standing start the athlete should position themselves such that the shin angle of the lead leg corresponds to the complete angle of extension that compliments that athletes output potential. The foot of the lead leg should be positioned just in front of the bottom dead centre line of the hips (if a vertical axis were to be drawn). The reason for this will be expounded upon in the next section.

The horizontal distance between the front and back foot should be approximately hip width and the longitudinal distance between the heel of the front foot and the instep of the back foot (as it will be positioned semi-horizontally in relation to the direction of take-off) must optimize the balance between the athlete having enough weight on the rear foot to push off yet not so much distance that it prolongs the time required to cycle the trail leg as it is the limb which establishes the first ground contact.

XIV.2.4. 3 AND 4 POINT LOW STARTS

3 and 4 point low starts will be discussed together due to the similarities shared between the two starting positions. The 4 point starting technique will be elaborated upon both with and without the use of starting blocks.

The thematic principles regarding front shin angle, line of extension, optimizing vertical and horizontal force application, and so forth that were discussed in the previous section apply equally to the scenarios of 3 and 4 point low starts. The difference being the kinematic starting positions themselves.

The kinematics of the 3 point start have often been a subject of debate amidst various coaching circles. Regarding a timed sprint, there are arguments surrounding the optimal position of the hand/arm that is not used for support, the proximity of the front foot in relation to the starting line, the proximity of both feet in relation to each other, the optimal hip height, and more. The answers to these questions are rooted in each athlete being able to satisfy the biomechanical truths that are impervious to debate.

The physics are undeniable and thus the question becomes how to satisfy the physical requirements relative to the particulars of each athlete. The universal truths are as follows:

- In the 3 point start, the athlete should position their support arm such that it forms a vertical axis into the ground. Athletes with greater upper body strength will be able to position the shoulder slightly forward of the hand; however, as the shoulder moves forward and in front of the hand the amount of load placed on the support arm/shoulder increases substantially. Alternatively, positioning the shoulder behind the hand is inefficient; as movement occurs (the shoulder passing over the hand) before the hand ever leaves the ground.

- The arm that is not in a position of support may mirror the the position of the support arm without actually exerting pressure into the ground. In this way, the arm is positioned to initiate the kinematic sequence of the take-off closer in proximity to the final overhead position.

- Alternatively, the athlete may demonstrate an effective start with the free arm cocked at their hip; however, the fact remains that the finalized position of that arm is overhead and by positioning it similar to the arm of support, such that it is free floating perpendicular to ground, it is that much closer to the final position yet still situated so as to allow for the propulsive initiation of the take-off.

Non-loaded arm hanging vertically

Non-loaded arm cocked at the hip

- The front foot, in contrast to what is often instructed, should be placed just behind the plum line of the crease in the hips. While this moves the foot farther way from the starting line, it also minimizes the movement amplitude required to achieve the subsequent extension while still allowing for adequate push off. The closer the front foot is placed to the starting line the more distance the hips must travel to pass the foot during extension. This creates a longer time interval to generate complete extension and the subsequent first ground contact.
- The horizontal distance between the two feet should be approximately shoulder width and the

placement of the rear foot, similar to the standing start, will differ from one athlete to the next based upon output ability and anthropometry. In all cases, however, the rear foot should be positioned such that it optimizes push off while minimizing the distance it must travel to make the first ground contact.

- The height of the hips in the set position is another frequently debated topic. Widely respected French T&F Coach Pierre Jean Vazel has explained this well. Regardless of the "set" position (the final static position held before take-off) the objective is for the hip height to gradually and smoothly increase up to the point of reaching maximum velocity. For this reason, the athlete must be mindful to set up in a position in which their hip height is not so high that they experience negative vertical hip displacement upon the first or second ground contact yet not so low that they cause themselves excess time to achieve extension during take-off.

The 4 point start without blocks follows nearly every point listed above with the exception of shoulder position in relation to the hands. In the 4 point start, with and without starting blocks, the shoulders may be positioned more forward of the hands in comparison to the 3 point start due to the fact that the load is distributed between both shoulders. The athlete must still be cautious not to move the shoulders too far in front of the hands as the excess downward pressure will slow the separation of the lead hand (which must thrust forward and up) from the running surface as well as shift the centre of mass farther away from what is optimal in regards to push off.

A great deal of data is available regarding the kinematics of the 4 point start with starting blocks. Some of the larger points are as follows:

- Front knee angle of 90-95 degrees
- Back knee angle of 120-130 degrees
- A common starting point for the front block placement is 2 foot lengths from the rearward edge of the starting line. In this way, when the athlete is in blocks, if they were to come down onto their front knee the knee should be on, or very close to, the starting line
- The rear block will typically be situated an additional .5 to 1 foot length behind the forward block.
- Similar to all other forms of starting, the most important thing is that the kinematics serve to equally complement the physics of overcoming static inertia in the horizontal direction as well

as the athlete's output ability and anthropometry.

Asafa Powell

In all starting positions it is suggested that the athletes either hold their breath as they exert the force of take-off or perform the valsalva manoeuvre (in which the air is very slowly released). This holds true throughout the bulk of the acceleration phase as greater intra-abdominal pressure is generated through either holding the lungs full of air or slowly releasing the pressure. This provides for greater stiffness through the torso which then serves as a more efficient transducer of the dynamic forces being generated by the arms and legs.

The diagnostic evaluations surrounding track athletes have been thorough to say the least. Certain studies have taken a look at the athletes sprint velocity in relation to breathing patterns and momentary drops in speed have been observed as having coincided with inhalation. In a timed short sprint it is then advantageous to either hold the air completely or slowly release the air until the distance is covered or the first inhalation is necessary. For example, a fit athlete is able to perform a 30-40 meter sprint on a single breath and elite 100m sprinters might take as few as 3 breaths to cover the entire race.

XIV.2.5. ACCELERATION + MAXIMUM VELOCITY

The impetus of optimizing the start is geared towards optimizing each successive step of the way. The acceleration phase is next in the order.

As previously discussed, a few of the universal biomechanical truths are positive shin angles during the initial steps (~4-5), a complete line of extension from shoulders to ankle with each step, and a body angle at takeoff and during acceleration that corresponds to that athletes output ability.

Stride length should be natural and not forced. During initial acceleration the force application/horizontal propulsion becomes reduced when an athlete attempts to elongate their stride beyond their naturally occurring output. This is made clear through the following practical example:

• Position yourself behind a parked car that is in neutral. Face forward with both hands on the vehicle and attempt to push it over 5 meters as fast as possible by taking as long as strides as possible. Note how awkward it feels to force the stride length and how much more difficult it is to overcome the car's static inertia in this way

It is not uncommon for untrained athletes to attempt to force their stride length in an effort to cover more ground and improve speed. The reality, however, is that, similar to the pitfalls of 'trying' to sprint faster, forcing stride length may actually reduce force application.

The positive shin angles that are central to initial acceleration become increasingly difficult to accomplish the more the athlete attempts to force stride length via airborne efforts versus greater force application into the ground. While the fastest sprinters spend more time in the air then their slower counterparts, the reason their flight times are greater is because they are applying more force, in less time, on the ground. Thus, provided reasonable flexibility is in place, stride length is a function of greater time dependent force application, as well as leg length, and not the athlete's attempt to take longer strides than what is biomechanically efficient.

The optimization of acceleration biomechanics entails that we revisit the physics of acceleration. Overcoming static inertia and subsequent acceleration requires that the line tangent to the curve of acceleration is as steep as possible. This signifies a high rate of force development. Provided the athlete has the physical qualities to produce a high rate of force development the degree to which this potential may be realized hinges upon the mechanical optimization of movement.

One may consider the optimal biomechanics of acceleration to exist as the story that best tells the kinematic path of transitioning from the start position to the upright sprint position in the most incrementally smooth way.

The proportionality of horizontal and vertical forces favours the horizontal during the start and initial acceleration then wains towards the vertical as the athlete reaches the upright position and the fastest speeds. At no time during a sprint, however, is the totality of force production owned by a single force vector.

The fact that the start and early acceleration favour the horizontal factors is what contributes to the muscle/mechanical 'pushing' effort. In this way, the physical sensation of starting and accelerating is distinct in comparison to sprinting at top speed.

Practical and pedagogical experience makes clear that the biomechanical optimization of acceleration is lead by the arms.

XIV.2.5.A. ARM ACTION

Of the volumes of track and field publications it is noteworthy to point out that the late Charlie Francis may have best described the neuromechanical implications of the arms on the sprint action as a whole. Charlie pointed out that the motor signal originates in the brain and the arms are closer in proximity to the brain then the legs. Thus, the signal reaches the arms first and the arm action must then play a decisive role in sprinting.

Practical experience as well as extensive analysis of the worlds elite sprinters, going back decades, reveals many commonalities shared between the most efficient "accelerators". Regarding the role of arm action, it serves a vital propulsive role as well as the essential role of counter rotation relative to the rotation that occurs around the hips from the leg action.

The degree of shoulder and elbow movement is not uniform throughout a sprint. Upon take-off from the start, or block clearance if starting blocks are used, the amplitude of arm movement about the shoulder and elbow during backside action is drastic and the movement amplitude during elbow extension incrementally reduces as the athlete approaches the upright position. Conversely, stride length incrementally increases with each stride up to the point of reaching maximum velocity.

Note the degree of elbow extension during the initial strides from Asafa Powell:

And how the amplitude of elbow extension is diminished as he approaches maximum velocity:

The backside movement amplitudes about the shoulder and elbow during initial acceleration are extreme, and must be extreme, in order to facilitate complete extension through the hips during ground contact. As the arm action provides the shoulder rotation which, while it presents counter rotation to the hips, enhances the rotation at the hip, the arm action indirectly influences stride length. As the hips rotate during knee lift each incremental degree of rotation increases the horizontal distance between the knee of the lead leg and the femur of the support leg. In this way, optimized arm action, and the associated hip rotation, offers an increase in stride length, however moderate, at a minimal muscle/mechanical cost.

During initial acceleration the arm action also influences the optimal position of the hips. If the arm action is too lethargic the hips will drift backwards, hinging, causing the chest to drift farther in front of bottom dead centre (the vertical axis through the hips). Not only does this inhibit complete extension and the associated lessening of force application, it also predisposes the athlete to stumbling because ground contact is occurring farther underneath the body.

The optimization of the arm action requires that the adjacent muscle compartments/antagonistic regions are as relaxed as possible. Herein lies the significance of relaxing the trapezius, neck, and facial muscles. For example, the misdirected nature of 'trying hard' to sprint fast frequently renders the athlete tightening up in favour of relaxing antagonist muscles; not the least of which are the trapezius, neck, and facial muscles. As the trapezius muscle, in particular, contracts it elevates the scapula and this restricts the achievable amplitude of shoulder movement as well as diminishes the elastic return following the back swing. While tightening the facial and neck muscles does not pose as direct a negative implication on arm action, it in no way presents an advantage.

Generally speaking, the elbows will flex to approximately 80-85 degrees in front and open to around 95-100 degrees in back; however, the degree of elbow extension during the back swing is resultant of force, not forebrain intention. The description of angles is for academic purposes only. The takeaways for coaches is that the hands should reach the level of the chin during frontside action and clear the hip during backside action. In so doing, the aforementioned angles of elbow flexion and extension will be achieved.

These joint angles reflect the optimization of lever length relative to power production:

- Too small a lever and the frequency is enhanced but at a loss of power- such as intentionally sprinting with as closed of an elbow position as possible.
- Too long a lever and power is enhanced but at a loss of frequency- such as intentionally sprinting with extended/straight arms.

As the arm action presents substantial implications on the stride, the athlete is well served to focus their attention on the optimal movement of the arms which is predicated on the downward action of the arm drive; which reinforces the stepping down action of the lead leg.

Arm action may be practiced in a variety of postures while the athlete is fixed in a static position. In this way, the significance of posture may be reinforced as the athlete gains valuable repetitions of practicing arm action. A favourable benefit of this exercise is the abdominal isometric endurance required to stabilize the torso from rotating about while driving the arms with the legs held static.

Coaching takeaway regarding arm action: down, down, down. Drive the hands down and allow the elastic return at the shoulder to take care of the rest.

XIV.2.5.B. POSTURE

The athlete should always make a point to maintain the anatomical position of the spine regardless of where they are in a sprint (starting position, early acceleration, transition, upright...). Extending the neck to look forward will prematurely cause the athlete to become upright; thereby diminishing acceleration.

The position/angle of the back, in relation to the ground, is what must dictate head/neck position; not the other way around. Thus, regardless if the athlete is taking off, accelerating, or in the upright position the position of the head/neck must be consistent with the position of the back throughout.

(Photo sequences taken from the 2012 NFL Combine preparation that I conducted for Rep 1 Sports Group. The athletes shown are Shea McClellin an Keshawn Martin. Shea was ultimately drafted as the 19th pick of the first round and currently starts for the Chicago Bears. Shea ran the 2nd fastest 40yd dash of all defensive linemen at the 2012 NFL Combine with a time of 4.63 at 260lb/~118kg bodyweight. Keshawn recorded a 4.45 40yd dash and one of the highest vertical jumps in the entire combine 39.5in/100.33cm. Keshawn was drafted in the 4th round to the Houston Texans and has remained an integral part of their starting lineup)

Extension at take-off

During Acceleration

In the upright position

During initial acceleration the athletes eyes should be fixed on a point on the ground that is 2-3 meters ahead. This will ensure that the head and neck position is inline with the back. Clearly, in team sports, the athletes eyes will be where the need to be; however, for the purposes of purely enhancing acceleration mechanics in order to sprint faster, the posture must be optimized.

XIV.2.5.C. LEG ACTION

It must be made clear that the focus on the proper mechanics of the arms will, to a great extent, promote an equivalent level of efficiency regarding the stride mechanics. This is because of the synchronicity that exists between the arms and legs during running.

Regarding the optimal biomechanics of the stride during acceleration, the applied physics section explained the propulsive factors- here we will discuss what to look for as well as cue, if necessary, regarding mechanics.

The significance of positive shin angles during initial acceleration was already discussed. This is one of the first mechanical factors to look for when an athlete is initiating a sprint from any static start; particularly a low start. The faster the athlete, particularly regarding their acceleration ability, the more steps they will take while maintaining positive shin angles at each ground contact. This is because their power output will allow them to maintain a shallower angle of extension at the take-off and early acceleration.

The strength of their muscular corset about the torso and general power output is what allows them to maintain shallower angles without falling on their face. A less strong/powerful athlete who tries to achieve an angle of extension that is too shallow for their ability will either stumble or fail to achieve complete extension. In this way, different from the instance in which lethargic arm action causes the hips to hinge, the hinging occurs because the athlete is intentionally bending forward during toe-off in a misplaced effort to stay low at the expense of incomplete extension and diminished force application.

Another misnomer that is popular amongst non-track coaches, who work with field sport athletes in developing sprint speed, is the idea that a large first step is optimal when starting from a 3 or

4 point low position. This can only be true if the athlete is explosive enough to take a large first stride and still achieve a positive shin angle upon ground contact.

- *One of top NFL kick returners between 2009 and 2012 was LaRod Stephens-Howling. I had the pleasure of coaching LaRod for two years at the university level as well as preparing him for his NFL Pro Day. Here he is shown accomplishing positive shin angles on the first 4 ground contacts subsequent to a low 3 point start on grass in preparation for his NFL pro day:*

Maximum extension at take-off

First 4 ground contacts with positive shin angles

Also important to point out is the maintenance of complete extension upon each subsequent toe-off:

Another Example from a Block Start- Complete extension upon take-off

Asafa Powell

Now, an example of **<u>what not to do</u>** from one of the fastest sprinters the world has ever known-Tyson Gay. Tyson owns the America Record in the 100m (9.69) and the second fastest 200m ran by an American (19.58).

Tyson, despite his incredible max velocity, and speed endurance; has always had trouble with his start and initial acceleration. One mechanical inefficiency that he routinely demonstrates during the initial strides is forcing a low angle with his torso at the expense of sacrificing complete extension during toe-off.

XIV.2.5.D. HEEL RECOVERY

Heel recovery refers to the action of the heel following toe-off and how close the heel approaches the buttocks and the subsequent collapse that occurs at the knee to create a shorter lever arm.

During the initial steps of acceleration the heel recovery will be relatively low, and in the case of certain sprinters such as Asafa Powell and Usain Bolt the recovery is so low following block clearance that the toe of the trail leg drags against the ground:

Notice the contrast between the heel recovery of Bolt and Tyson Gay

The subject of the toe drag has been controversial amongst track coaches and analysts. In any case, the comparatively low heel recovery during initial acceleration (regardless if the toe drags or not) has to do with the fact that the force vector is so heavily weighed in favour of the horizontal that efficiency is optimized by minimizing the vertical displacement created by the path of the foot as it travels through the recovery cycle. The main point is driving the knee forward.

Note the low degree of heel recovery demonstrated by Asafa Powell during his first step out of the blocks:

First Step:

Compare the height of Powell's foot relative to the knee of the support leg during initial acceleration out of the blocks against the height as it passes the support leg in the upright position.

As the athlete continues to proceed through the acceleration phase the heel recovery will become more pronounced in terms of the vertical displacement; regarding the highest level sprinters. The higher heel recovery shortens the lever arm of the leg and, as a result, places less mechanical stress on the flexors of the hip to bring the leg forward during the recovery cycle. This is more efficient at this point in the sprint in which the vertical force vector is dramatically more pronounced due to the sprinter's posture and the height at which the foot falls from prior to stepping down.

An oversimplification of the stride dynamics would be to state that acceleration is a matter of pushing across while maximum velocity is a matter of stepping down; when in actuality both horizontal and vertical forces are present at all times.

The term 'toe over knee' is illustrated in the following photos; reflective of the position of the foot of the recovery leg as it passes by the knee of the support leg.

Bolt, Lemaitre, and Tyson Gay are excellent examples of sprinters who have phenomenal heel recovery (note how the recovery leg is collapsed at the knee):

While the degree of heel recovery during sprinting is not the sole contributing factor towards elite results, it is in every way a mechanical advantage. The suppleness of the musculo-tendonous apparatus about the thigh and knee are intrinsic to this ability and surely muscular bulk will inhibit the degree to which the heel may approach the buttocks. Thus, genetic and morphological factors surely play a role; however, the efficacy of manual therapy cannot be ignored in regards to its positive influence on joint mobility.

XIV.2.5.E. PENDULUM- FRANS BOSCH

Biomechanist Frans Bosch has elucidated upon a paramount biomechanical truth shared by the fastest sprinters in the world- the pendulum. This characterizes the orientation of the two legs during the flight phase at top speed in terms of the amplitude of the pendulum/scissor action that occurs between the two.

The desirability of the reduced amplitude pendulum may seem counterintuitive at first; however, the significance of it reinforces the fact that stride length is not merely a function of separating the legs; but rather, generating more time specific force at ground contact and the resultant enhanced flight time.

Further, the importance of limiting the degree to which the knee of the trail leg passes the hips moving backwards after toe- off is linked to minimizing the mechanical workload of the sprint as a whole. While a more elongated muscle carries greater elastic energy, such as the thigh of the trail leg extending further behind the hips, it also requires more energy to execute movement over a greater working amplitude (driving the knee forward).

XIV.2.5.F. POSITION OF THE FOOT PRIOR TO GROUND CONTACT

Prior to ground contact the knee extends and the ankle remains relatively neutral in order to pre-load the achilles tendon. This enhances the elastic return during ground contact as well as minimizes movement/deformation (via increased stiffness) about the ankle; thereby lessening ground contact time.

Common coaching cues are 'toe up' in reference to the dorsiflexion of the first metatarsal.

Note the position of the foot just prior to ground contact of Bolt, Powell, and Lemaitre:

XIV.2.6. THE BIOMECHANICAL TRUTHS OF SPRINTING

When problem solving it is prudent to first assume a global perspective and then initiate the process of deconstruction down to the basal level. The biomechanical truths that have previously been discussed serve as the elemental movement components of sprinting. These basal constituents are impervious to debate and are thus key focus areas for coaches and athletes to direct their attention towards during the preparation. The primary biomechanical truths of sprinting are summarized below:

- When initiating a start from a static position ensure that the orientation of the feet, hips, and centre of mass are situated in order to accommodate the athletes power output and anthropometric proportions

- When taking off from a low position the kinematic sequence is initiated by the arm contralateral to the rearward leg

- The position of the head and neck must be consistent with the position of the back throughout

- The sprint action is heavily influenced by the arms

- The emphasis of arm action should be down, down, down

- While the angle about the elbow will change during frontside and backside action, the objective should be to hold a position of approximately 90 degrees and allow the forces at work to take care of the rest

- A complete line of extension from the shoulders down to the ankles is the objective at toe off and the angle of extension relative to the ground, during acceleration, must correspond to the athletes output ability

- Positive shin angles during initial strides are central towards optimal acceleration from the start

- The transition from acceleration to upright sprinting should be smooth and not forced

- While all great sprinters run with high knees in the upright position the focus should be on stepping down

- By focusing on flexing the big toe up, when stepping down, he athlete will establish optimal foot position prior to ground contact

- A short acceleration, less than 30-40m, should be completed on a single breath that is either held throughout or slowly released in order to maximize stiffness through the torso

- The pendulum is optimized, during upright sprinting, when the rearward travel of the support leg, after toe-off, is minimal

XIV.3. APPLIED PHYSIOLOGY

This section will discuss the bioenergetic contributions to sprinting.

There is no clearer explanation of bioenergetic parameters than that which was explained by Tsvetan Zhelyaskov and Daniela Dasheva of the National Sports Academy in Sofia Bulgaria in their landmark publication "Training and Adaptation in Sport". The following text, in italic, has been taken from that book:

The energy criteria for the trained state of the organism are related to three types of energy production capabilities: aerobic, anaerobic-glycolytic, and anaerobic-alactic. On this basis the following indicators are developed for the respective particular criteria:

Indicator for the power*- this is the maximal amount of energy per unit time that can be provided by each of the indicated sources. It is determined by the respective particular criteria:*
- *For the aerobic power- the maximal oxygen consumption and the critical power of work, where maximal oxygen utilization is reaches;*
- *For the glycolytic power- the lactate oxygen debt related to the work time, and the maximal increase of lactic acid in blood, excess CO2, changes in the blood buffering properties;*
- *For the alactic power- the alactacid oxygen, the breakdown of CP (creatine phosphate) in working muscles, etc*

Indicator for the capacity*- this is the total work output that can be provided by one or another source of energy. Its particular criteria are:*
- *For the capacity of the aerobic processes- the total amount of oxygen uptake above the resting level throughout the whole duration of work, and the product of the critical power and the total work time;*
- *For the glycolytic capacity- the magnitude of the lactacid oxygen debt, the amount of lactate during work, CO2 release and the buffering reserves of blood;*
- *For the alactic capacity- the magnitude of the oxygen debt and the total CP stores in the muscles.*

Indicator for the efficiency- *this is the ratio of the directly measurable energy cost and the magnitude of performed work (or the ration of the maximal oxygen uptake to the critical work power). The criteria for the efficiency of the respective processes can be the ratios of work power during lactacid and alactacid oxygen debt.*

Physiologically, if we revert back to the time:motion data of Bolt and Powell during the 2009 Berlin WC we know that 90% of acceleration is accomplished in the first 30m. This is nearly entirely anaerobic-alactic because it is so short in duration, less than 4 seconds in their case, (so short that the work bout may be completed on a single breath) and very high in intensity relative to the meters per second in which both men were traveling. Their capacity for acceleration is what allows them to cover so much ground in so little time; however, all men where not created equal and, as a result, time is of the essence in relation to how much ground may be covered in a certain period.

XIV.3.1. TIME IS OF THE ESSENCE

Regarding a continuous effort, the bioenergetic contribution is dependent upon the intensity of the work bout relative to the time, or duration, of the event.

In the case of sprinting, the faster the speed the more ground that is covered per unit time. In this way, provided intensity is maximal, the alactic period is dependent upon the athlete's speed potential and as speed is developed- so is the alactic threshold.

Consider, once again, the 100m final at the 2009 T&F World Championship in Berlin. Bolt reached his max velocity at 70m in 7.10s and Powell reached his at 60m in 6.39s. Bolt's superior speed allowed him to not only cover more ground in less time; but also to continue to accelerate over a longer distance for a longer period of time. Maximal acceleration can only happen in an alactic environment. In this way, Bolt's alactic threshold is farther to the right, on the timeline, in comparison to Powell's. As a result, the bioenergetic proportionality of Bolt's race included a lesser lactic component in comparison to Powell's.

Herein lies additional support for the alactic speed + extensive tempo argument for team based field sports. By pushing the alactic threshold farther to the right not only does the lactic contribution to a sustained/continuous effort become reduced, within a fixed period such as the 100m distance, it also becomes reduced regarding the successive repetition of sub-maximal speed intervals- such as those which constitute team based field sports. This is because the enhanced speed reserve pushes previous sub-maximal efforts further into the sub-maximal realm.

Consider an athlete whose max velocity in a 30m sprint is 8m/s and during a game the bulk of 20-30m distances are covered at 6.5m/s. The 6.5m/s represents 81% of the athletes max V.

After an off-season of alactic speed work the athlete improves their speed to the point that they reach 8.5m/s in a 30m sprint. Now, the corporate average 6.5m/s represents 76% of their current max V.

The increased speed reserve has pushed the corporate average running repeats further into the sub-maximal domain and, coupled with intelligently structured aerobic workloads, thereby created a lesser physiological demand. Furthermore, the increased speed allows the athlete to cover a greater distance, with maximal intensity, and still remain within the alactic period.

XIV.3.2. BIOENERGETIC TRAINING PARAMETERS

The following table illustrates various training parameters for the bioenergetic systems. The data has been compiled based upon the work of Yuri Verkhoshansky, Vladimir Issurin, Victor Seluyanov, and Charlie Francis:

Type of Training	Training Intensity	Duration of Set	Rest Between Sets	Number of Sets
Anaerobic alactic Power	Maximum	<6sec	2-5min	5-6
	High	10-20sec	3min	5-7
Anaerobic alactic Capacity	Maximum	7-10sec	30s-1.5min	10-12
	High	10-20sec	1.5-2min	4
	High	10sec	10sec	6-10
Anaerobic glycolytic Power	High	20-30sec	6-10min	3-4
	Moderate	30-50sec	2-3min	3-4
Anaerobic glycolytic Capacity	High	40-90sec	5-6min	10-15
	High	60sec	3min	6-8
	High	20-30sec	20-30sec	6-10
	Moderate	60sec	1-2min	3-4
Aerobic Power	*Max VO$_2$	30s-2.5min	30s-3min	10-15
	High	60sec	40-60sec	8
	Increasing	3min	3min	3-6
Aerobic Capacity	*Max VO$_2$	1-6min	1-6min	>10
	High	40sec	20sec	10-12
	Fartlek	*5min@AnT+20s	varied	5-10
	Uniform	20-60min	-	Varied
	Moderate	15-30sec	30-60sec	10-20

*Max VO$_2$ signifies the work level intensity at the limit of the athletes' capacity to transport and utilize oxygen to fuel the incremental increase in intensity level of exercise. Max VO$_2$ is determined in vitro by means of sophisticated laboratory equipment.

*5min@AnT+20s = (5minutes of exercise at the anaerobic threshold concluded with a 20 second surge at a higher intensity level intermixed with intervals of moderate intensity exercise)

While the directive of this publication is geared towards applied sprint training, the parameters illustrated in the table may be applied to any form of repeated movement and are thus applicable for the spectrum of competitive sports.

Specifically in regards to alactic speed training, the following guidelines (volumes per session) have stood the test of time and have been taken from the work of Charlie Francis:

Distance	Effort	Reps	Total
<30m	Maximal	6-8	180-240m
50m	Maximal	5-6	250-300m
60m	Maximal	4-6	240-360m

In regards to alactic speed training, the recoveries between attempts must be complete. Not all working efforts are created equal; and terrestrial sprint efforts are as high in neuromuscular intensity as any action that a human being is capable of generating. For this reason, the recovery intervals between alactic sprint efforts must be substantial.

Recall the description of alactic power which characterizes the peak intensity of the system. The complete biochemical restitution of ATP-CP must occur in order to preserve the peak intensity of efforts and ensure that each consecutive rep is of equal quality; both in terms of output as well as mechanical integrity. A general rule for recovery times, between alactic power sprint efforts, is 1minute for every 10meters up to 60 meters:

- 10m- 1-2minutes
- 20m- 2-3minutess
- 30m- 3-4minutes
- 40m- 4-5minutes

- 50m- 5-6minutes
- 60m- 6-8minutes

The recovery times for speed endurance and special endurance efforts, while they are not alactic efforts, become exceedingly longer; yet, for the same reason- in order to ensure that peak intensity is achieved on every repetition conducted in training with no deterioration in intensity on subsequent attempts.

- Speed Endurance runs 80- 150m or 8-15sec of maximal intensity may be separated by recoveries as long as 15-20minutes (regarding 120-150m efforts)
- Special Endurance I (150-300m or 15-45sec) and II (300-600m or +45sec) runs may feature recoveries as long as 30-45minutes between individual repetitions
- The rest interval exception to the special endurance runs is linked to the split runs that are specific to short to long programs. In this case, the rest between segments of a split run will be incomplete; however, the recoveries between sets may be comparable to that of the continuous runs specific to a long to short

The instances in which recoveries will be incomplete by design is in order to challenge the capacity of the bioenergetic system; however, the quality of each successive repetition must be preserved, and not deteriorate, as both the movement output and biomechanical efficiency are central to all training.

When addressing the alactic capacity, or any other bioenergetic requirement, for various sports, most notably the team based field and court sports, it is useful to review the time: motion research (or conduct your own if it is not available) and perform a deconstruction of the highest intensity movement bracket into the appropriate set, repetition, and work interval schemes. For example: Roberts, Stokes, and Trewartha (2008) conducted a comprehensive time: motion assessment of elite rugby union in their publication- *The Physical Demands of Elite English Rugby Union.* A portion of that data is presented here:

Time: Motion Data						
Total distance (m) travelled in each activity category (mean + s)						
	Forwards			Backs		
Category	Tight Forwards	Loose Forwards	All Forwards	Inside Backs	Outside Backs	All Backs
Standing	355 ± 52	352 ± 53	354 ± 50	317 ± 22	272 ± 82b	293 ± 63a
Walking	1840 ± 224	2045 ± 208	1928 ± 234	2161 ± 155b	2517 ± 277b,c,d	2351 ± 287a
Jogging	1985 ± 466	2075 ± 326	2024 ± 400	2094 ± 224	1936 ± 418	2010 ± 340
MI Running	807 ± 225	819 ± 218	812 ± 214	917 ± 164	725 ± 223d	815 ± 215
HI Running	275 ±114	327 ± 98	298 ± 107	439 ± 107	456 ± 185	448 ± 149a
Sprinting	144 ±189	192 ± 203	164 ± 189	124 ± 78	280 ± 185	207 ± 185
Total	5408 ± 702	5812 ± 666	5581 ± 692	6055 ± 455	6190 ± 929	6127 ± 724a
a Significantly different to forwards, P50.05.						
b Significantly different to tight forwards, P50.05.						
c Significantly different to loose forwards, P50.05.						
d Significantly different to inside backs, P50.05.						

Using this data, as only one example, one may extrapolate the appropriate bracket and corresponding volume range per position and then dissect that specific volume of running into a series of sets, reps, and rest intervals for the purposes of a sprint or aerobic interval session. For example:

- Loose forwards conducted a range of 192m plus or minus 203m worth of sprinting per match

- Taking the highest possible volume of 395meters (192 + 203), one may reasonable target an alactic capacity session to include 395 rounded up to 400 total meters of alactic sprint repeats as a final training session during pre-competition season preparations.

- Between the jogging (which does not necessitate a designated training load), medium and high intensity running (which in most studies exists beneath 6m/s) one may work with a total extensive tempo volume as low as 1150m. This would logically be advanced to the range of 2000-2400m as 1150m is so low and the extensive tempo is a low intensity variable to begin with; however, as alactic capacity stresses the oxidative properties of the fast twitch muscle fibres the tempo volume need not escalate once the training of alactic capacity begins. In fact, it may reduce proportionally as the volume of alactic capacity increases.

- The off-season period would then dictate that the coach work backwards from that number in order to establish the appropriate loading sequence per week and per session

- As alactic capacity is a function of alactic power it is logical to precede an alactic capacity training block with the development of pure alactic power.

XV. SPECIALIZED EXERCISES

The value of specialized exercises, in the preparation of any athlete, cannot be overstated. In fact, one would not be negligent in stating that the scope of physical load that is possible to be occupied by specialized movement is the most significant contribution to athlete preparation. Ironically, however, this aspect of movement preparation, properly executed and organized in the overall plan, is absent in the preparation of most athletes.

Specialized exercises are based upon the biomotor, biodynamic, and bioenergetic structure of the competition exercise. Regarding sprint training, we know the following (for purposes of explanation- the biodynamics category references the knee angles during the position of ground support):

	Biomotor	Biodynamic	Bioenergetic
Static Start (Block Start)	Starting/acceleration strength	Front knee angle of 90-95 degrees Back knee angle of 120-130 degrees	Anaerobic-alactic/ATP-CP
Acceleration	Explosive/RFD/reactive/elastic	1st step 85-95 degrees, increasing each step	Anaerobic-alactic/ATP-CP
Maximum Velocity	RFD/Reactive/ elastic	Finalizes at 165-170 degrees	Anaerobic-alactic/ATP-CP
Speed Endurance	Reactive/ elastic	165-170 degrees	Anaerobic-Lactic
Special Endurance I	Reactive/ elastic	165-170 degrees	Anaerobic-Lactic/Aerobic
Special Endurance II	Reactive/ elastic	165-170 degrees	Anaerobic-Lactic/Aerobic

From this we may make strong arguments for the following specialized exercises according to biomotor, biodynamic, and bioenergetic characteristics. The degree to which specialized exercises benefit the competition skill is referred to as 'transfer' or 'correspondence'. Honoured Russian Throws coach, and former Olympic champion in the hammer, Anatoliy Bondarchuk has authored comprehensive texts on the transfer of training.

From the table we know that we are accounting for biomotor activity, the angle of the knee during ground support, and the bioenergetic contribution to that aspect of the sprint.

Following are viable examples of specialized exercises for the block start, acceleration, and maximum velocity phases of a sprint, not including the direct practice of each aspect itself; given the factors presented in the previous table :

XV.1. BLOCK START

Highest Degree of Transfer

- Static overcome by ballistic single response jumps and implement throws from angles of knee bend no less than 80 degrees; from position of double leg support; with the possibility of varied stagger positions between feet
- Static overcome by explosive barbell squats from angles of knee bend no less than 80 degrees; sub-maximal loads that allow for high rate of force development
- Explosive, Sub-max static overcome by dynamic Cleans, Pulls, and Snatches from starting knee bend positions no less than 80 degrees of flexion

Secondary Transfer

- Any single effort static overcome by ballistic implement throws and jumps
- Any single effort static overcome by explosive resistance exercises involving hip and knee extension

XV.2. ACCELERATION

The bioenergetic contribution to acceleration is relatively stable throughout; however, the biomotor contribution evolves from explosive to reactive elastic and the biodynamic factor of the angle of knee flexion during ground support changes with each step. These considerations must be factored into the specialized exercises in terms of the method of execution.

Highest Degree of Transfer

- Hill and sled sprints in which the velocity is within 5-10% of the athletes velocity on flat ground without external resistance for the same acceleration distance; up to 6 seconds in duration

Secondary Transfer

- Single and Multiple response explosive horizontal jumps with knee bend angles ranging between 80-90 degrees for early acceleration up to 150-160 degrees for late acceleration. These jumps may be executed up hill, up stairs, or on flat ground for up to 6 seconds

- Same leg, RRLL, and RLRL bounds up hill, up stadium stairs, or on flat ground with the appropriate degrees of knee bend during ground support; up to 6 seconds

- Explosive skips for distance; up to 6 seconds

- Any number of hip, hip/knee, hip/knee/ankle extension resistance exercises performed with the appropriate degree of knee bend and explosive muscle contraction; up to 6 seconds

XV.3. MAXIMUM VELOCITY

Highest Degree of Transfer

- Flying Sprints in which the pre-run is long enough and corresponds to that athletes requirements to reach maximum velocity in a more relaxed fashion and the window of max V is 10-20meters as that is the accepted distance over which max V may be sustained

- Speed Change Drills (fast-easy-fast and easy-fast-easy), the most common method of performing these is over segments that are 20m, or more, in length and correspond to that athlete's speed potential. 20M + 20m + 20m for a total distance of 60m. It is critical that the transition between segments is very smooth and largely influenced by volitional changes in arm action. The differential in intensity will be relatively small ~5%. In this way the easy sections will be approximately 90% intensity and the fast sections approximately 95% intensity.

Secondary Transfer

- Single and Multiple response jumps with a vertical emphasis, minimized knee bend/ground contact times, and performed within the alactic period, such as:
    - Hurdle hops in which the hurdles a placed relatively close (~1meter) with the heights adjusted to each athletes reactive/elastic ability
    - Depth jumps less than .75m or what corresponds to each athletes strength preparation and reactive/elastic ability
    - Skip bounds with a vertical push-off emphasis

XVI. ALACTIC SPEED WORK

Featured on Jimson Lee's www.speedendurance.com

"There's nothing more elusive than an obvious fact" Sir Arthur Conan Doyle

The increase in maximum velocity is the most important training component for any short sprinter as they progress through their career. Casual observations reveal, however, that the training problem for a vast population of sprinters is that too few are exposed to intelligently structured work: rest schemes, training load taxonomy, and a sufficient volume of alactic speed development.

The approach of initiating training years with low intensity and large volumes of running quickly outlives its usefulness due to the need for the short sprinter to attain ever increasing meters per second.

The "incomplete" long to short approach, in which training years begin with either completely unrelated middle distance runs or slightly more relevant 300-600m special endurance runs, void of supplementary acceleration and maximum velocity sprint volumes, fails to most effectively address the sprinter's need to develop more speed.

Further, the antiquated approach of initiating a short sprinters training year with high volumes of slower runs causes detrimental adaptations at the muscular level. The lactic stress of the special endurance runs, void of the presence of vital alactic work, causes great stress to the intra-cellular lactate buffer mechanisms. This stress results in the adaptive consequence of red fiber behavior at the level of the valuable white fiber; which then, diminishes high velocity contractile capacity. It is for this reason why, on average a thrower will out jump a sprinter.

The shorter the event duration the greater the explosive demand and the greater the proportion of that specialist's training load volume is directed towards alactic/explosive/strength efforts. The consequential adaptation is seen at the muscular level in which the most profound explosive ability is seen in athletes who utilize the greatest proportion of their training load towards alactic/explosive developmental protocols.

This phenomenon is also evident on a purely intuitive level: adaptation is essentially a defense/survival reaction within the body. Stress is incurred and, depending on its magnitude, the body generates an appropriate defense reaction. It is therefore intuitive that the body's response to the most explosive sorts of stressors is to develop explosive ability. Alternatively, the defense reaction to longer/slower/less explosive stress will not be relevant to a short sprinter if not accompanied by alactic stress.

With each passing year there must be a gradually sloped intensification of the training load, increased therapy schedule, and the associated volumes of acceleration and maximum velocity sprints, in order to provide the stimulus necessary to promote the needed adaptations for the short sprinter; though surely not limited to short sprinters.

This logic applies regardless of whether the chosen methodological approach is long to short, short to long, or an aggregate of the two. In all cases, every subsequent training year must be initiated, in part, with acceleration development work and lead towards, either down from (in the case of L-S) or up to (in the case of S-L) the maximum velocity intensity ranges.

Special endurance runs, while necessary for a +200m sprinter (but certainly not for a 100m sprinter), alone, do not positively affect speed development once the sprinter has reached a reasonable level of performance.

It is a function of differentials.

If a developing male sprinter is generating 10.5 m/s in the 100m race and is capable of going 9.5m/s over a 300m run then it is rational to suggest that the special endurance run will provide sufficient stimulation to advance his pure speed. This is because 9.5m/s represents an excess of 90% of his maximum velocity. On the other hand, a world class sprinter who is capable of 11.8m/s over a 100m is highly unlikely to advance speed based upon special endurance runs alone because the differential between what he's likely able to average over the 300m (possibly 10.5 m/s) and his maximum velocity is too great.

Thus, regarding the world class level, the associated special endurance velocities are too low and speed is a one way street. Sprinting at +12m/s does, in every way, suggest that the Usain Bolt's, Asafa Powell's, Tyson Gay's, Ben Johnson's, Carl Lewis', Donovan Bailey's,... of the world are capable of running sub 20sec in the 200m. In no way, however, does running 19.80 in the 200m or sub 32sec in the 300m, for example, suggest that the sprinter is capable of making 12m/s in the 60-80m range and running sub 9.8 sec in the 100m.

Increased speed provides for a valuable speed reserve for the longer sprints. Usain Bolt was able to go 19.19 in the 200m because he went 9.58 in the 100m. Michael Johnson was able to go 43.18 in the 400m because because he could go 19.32 in the 200m and sub 10.10 in the 100m. Marita Koch was able to go 47.60 in the 400m because she could go sub 22 in the 200m and 10.83 in the 100m . It is only in the presence of this type of speed capability that the value of special endurance takes its place at the sprint training round table.

In short, it doesn't matter what level of speed a sprinter can maintain regardless of how fast they can't sprint (take note team sport coaches who overload their athletes with speed endurance and special endurance runs).

Task specific work capacity may only be developed via task specific training. It is the accumulated exposure to task specific training, over the course of a training year, which builds the special work capacity and renders the sprinter more able to attain multiple peaks over the course of a competition calendar; and more resilient to the stress of maximal and near maximal velocities. The appropriate and carefully monitored dosage of task specific training, over time, is vital for all athletes as the exposure to it normalizes the stress. For a short sprinter, task specific training is training at or near maximum velocity.

The simple rule of long term sprint development is that one must train fast in order to become fast. This requires a re-formatted training week which provides for the necessary recovery/regeneration opportunities and intensification of the training load.

This holds true regardless of level of qualification. School age/high school age sprinters, in particular, require proper exposure to alactic speed because transitional muscle fiber essentially ceases to be plastic post puberty. A young teenage sprinter, and any other speed/power athlete, who is not exposed to sufficient volumes of alactic speed work will not develop the vital muscular adaptations necessary to attain world class results later in life.

As for world class sprinters who have developed their speed following a one dimensional linear approach; beginning with special endurance , only, and gradually intensifying the load as the competition season approaches- genetic gifts are much like diplomatic immunity; they provide the irresponsible user with a sizeable degree if impunity; regardless of the nature of their actions.

XVII. APPLIED SPRINT TRAINING
IMPLICATIONS ON ENHANCING SPORT SKILL EXECUTION FOR NON-TRACK ATHLETES
Featured on Jimson Lee's www.speedendurance.com

Three coaching perspectives may be considered in the endeavor to enhance the speed and execution of competition maneuvers of non-track athletes, that of the track coach, the technical-tactical coach, and the conditioning coach; and in all cases, the individual must understand applied sprint training.

Any track coach knows that a sprint champion was never created in the weight room; and that all work done off the track can only serve as a means toward the greater ends which exists on the track. While weights, and strength training in general, may play a vital supplement in a sprinters preparation; they must remain in the background. Exceptions are limited to sprinters who are restricted in their preparation to extreme cold weather environments with limited or no indoor running space; however, a sub-9.8second 100m man has yet to emerge from such a place so take that for what it's worth in terms of what can be accomplished void of more optimal training conditions.

Historically, a track coach was one of the prime examples of a programme manager in that he or she was the sole authority who governed over the near totality of physical loading sustained by the athletes.

This status is preserved in most cases at the club and high school (primary/secondary) level; however, since the institution of the S&C realm of coaching the loading experienced by many collegiate track athletes has risen.

All the training variables being under the programming and organizational supervision of the same person presents measurable advantages. Technical-tactical loads (track work), as well as all other loading (jumps, throws, weights, calisthenics, ...) are strategically planned (intensities, volumes, densities, ...). The result is highly predictable training and race outcomes. Knowing this, it is evident that knowledge of track, as well as field, training strategies are highly beneficial for the programme management preparation of non-track athletes who similarly must peak for competitions.

In non-track, particularly team sports, however, the misnomer has been popularized that the peaking of physical readiness and player execution ability is out of reach.

141

Technical-tactical coaches are, to the detriment of their athletes, typically not required to understand sport physiology or biomechanics. Thus, actual technical know how (applied biomechanics) and physical loading strategies are qualities that would greatly enhance the skill set of technical-tactical coaches . Alternatively, what has and continues to stand at the forefront of 'coaching education' in this realm is the study and advancement of tactics. While a technical-tactical coach, head coach, is theoretically in a position to programme manage, the list of other responsibilities that often comes with the job, particularly at the higher levels, would prove such a task difficult and beyond the skill set of most candidates due to their incomplete education.

Due to the predominant stress of tactical understanding, and not technical or physiological, many technical-tactical trainings are planned void of accounting for the physiological implications of the work. It is for this reason, in particular, why many pre-season training camps, regardless of sport yet surely highlighted by team sports, feature some of the highest instance of non-contact related traumas.

Conditioning coaches exist in the periphery regardless of sport and thus any loading he or she presents is in excess to what is already occurring in the technical-tactical realm. The obvious exception are off-seasons, which differ in length and kind according to sport, in which technical-tactical loading is reduced or kept to a minimum. Conditioning coaches "should", however, make candidates for programme managers in that they "should" possess the requisite knowledge of training load programming and organization; however, many coaching education curricula fail to provide this type of global understanding of sport physiology/biomechanics in favor of the more narrow scope of exercise physiology. This is illogical even void of the concept of programme management as knowledge of exercise science/physiology, as most curricula are administered, tells us nothing about sport science/physiology.

Track and technical-tactical coaches typically view training from an outside – in perspective (ergo the track, field, court, is outside of the weight room and therefore track, field, court work is prioritized), while most conditioning coaches education and subsequent practice typically works from the inside – out (weight room first then everything else). This is, in part, because educational curriculums are flawed and many coaches take the words far too literally within their practice. This is stated because while certain sports/disciplines require more in the realm of muscular strength and force outputs than others, there are no sports/disciplines which rely solely upon work done in the weight room other than Olympic weightlifting, Powerlifting, and Strongman.

Ultimately, it stands to reason that the optimal approach is neither outside in or inside out- but rather all encompassing/global.

Knowledge of sprint training is an excellent means of understanding the global concept of programme management and how it may be applied to the realm of non-track athlete sports.

Technical-tactical loading for non-track athletes may be viewed analogous to a sprinters track work in that it is the most relevant form of training to the sport results themselves. During periods of time when technical-tactical loading is being performed in appreciable volumes (training camps, pre-seasons, competition calendars), the conditioning coach must take care in ensuring that any additional loading is complimentary and compatible to the technical-tactical load. In the case of speed work, one must consider what is already being done in sport practice and what sort of speed work, if any, might be useful in addition.

Late Canadian sprint coach Charlie Francis used the glass of water analogy to describe this very phenomena in the context of sprint training and additional CNS intensive loading. Fill up the glass with an abundance of one and there is little room left for another because CNS resources are finite. Overflow the glass and the athlete is trashed.

The sprint actions in the vast majority of non-track sports, played on a field, court or ice, are limited to short accelerations; most of which are less than 30meters. For this reason, if it is determined that additional speed work is justified during a period of technical-tactical loading, it makes sense to look at how that may be accomplished.

From a programme management standpoint, which is by far the most efficient course of action, the technical-tactical loading is adjusted, from a proportionality standpoint, in order to ensure that the largest portion of high to maximum intensity running is reserved for the speed work itself. In this way, the remainder of technical-tactical loading is restricted to sub-maximal realms of intensity (that do not conflict with the speed work) which offer a broad range of possibilities including but not limited to movement outputs related to power speed, aerobic intervals of competition maneuvers, and strictly technical work that is limited in physical output (all of which provide excellent means of low cost-higher volume training and associated exposure to skill advancement opportunities).

From a physical preparatory standpoint, in which the technical-tactical loading is fixed and not open for debate, the trainer must exact any additional sprint loading (in terms of method of execution as well as volume) with surgical precision. In this way, considering there is already an appreciable volume of accelerations being performed as part of sport practice the options are as follows:

For the purposes of speed development in the presence of technical-tactical loading provided the athletes already possess sufficient sprint mechanics:

- Flying sprints- by offering a longer yet sub-maximally initiated approach run they provide for greater energy stores to be available at maximum velocity. A short maximal velocity window of 10-20 meters then limits the breadth of exposure and will, to varying degrees, exceed any speeds reached in the technical-tactical practice. In the context of technical-tactical loading, a small overall volume of these runs is suitable due to their heightened intensity- and by association, risk to muscular trauma. In a given session (preceding technical-tactical practice yet on the same day) a suggested dose of these sprints is no more than 3-6, depending on length, and experience has shown that the length of the pre-run may be as short as 15-20meters (for athletes of low speed preparation and/or large bodymass) up to 40-60meters for athletes of high speed preparation and output. Most field sport athletes will do well with no more than a 30m approach run.

For the purposes of ground based reactive/elastic and explosive locomotive output in the presence of technical-tactical loading:

- Jumps up and off, jumps up + up and off, jumps up stairs, jumps up hill- in all cases the ground impact forces are reduced due to the ever increasing height of the support apparatus. The repeated nature of the efforts, in comparison to single response efforts, introduces the reactive/elastic component and provided the geometry of the 'obstacles' (boxes, slope of stairs, dimension of stairs, slope of hill) are suitable, the athletes are unrestricted in their ability to volitionally generate output (even though, similar to hill and sled sprints, the actual intensity of the output is reduced).

- All of the jump variants should involve deeper knee bends. The greater degree of knee flexion during repeated jump efforts the greater the correlation to acceleration mechanics in which the knee is more flexed during ground contact due to the position of the body.

- While these jumps will not do much to enhance technical abilities related to sprinting, the can serve a very interesting role in developing reactive/elastic and explosive qualities of the hips and legs which are closely related to acceleration ability; and in appropriate volumes they are very manageable to perform during technical-tactical loading periods while posing no conflict.

For the purposes of acceleration development as a skill in the presence of technical-tactical loading:

- Hill Sprints- by virtue of running up a hill (preferably of low to moderate incline) the anti-gravitational effort reduces speed output (intensity) without the expense of reduced volitional effort. The reduced intensity allows for a greater volume of work to be performed of a non-conflicting nature (greater volumes then allow for more opportunity to enhance skill). The hill also offers an advantage in terms of reduced stress to the hamstrings as the athlete is kept in a position of acceleration in which the movement dynamics of the legs are quadricep dominant. In this way, the distance would typically be kept to less than 30meters. Restricting recoveries is another means of reducing intensity. Similar to the flying sprints, the total number of sprints performed preceding a sport practice would vary according to the length of the run.

- Sled Sprints- the sled, provided the overload does not diminish the athletes speed by a wide margin, offers very similar benefits as the hill (in terms of reduced intensity without reduced effort as well as lessened hamstring involvement due to the acceleration position) and thus the loading parameters are the same.

- In both cases, the hill or the sled enhance acceleration mechanics by default if only with respect to posture (the resistance causes the athletes to assume a body angle closer to the ground and accelerate as fast as possible). This can subvert the need for the coach to go over that, and the associated cues (knees through, push into the ground..) that might be necessary when performing unresisted sprints on the flat. To this it becomes essential to instruct and monitor arm mechanics and head position.

- While both hill and sled runs may effectively be performed well beyond the 30m mark for a variety of reasons, it is suggested to limit the distances to 30m for the purposes of acceleration development
- In the context of a progammme management scenario, or under the supervision of a conditioning coach, these forms of sprint training, dosed properly, may effectively be performed during periods of technical-tactical loading while posing no conflict.

Provided time constraints are not limiting, it is even manageable to perform low volumes of these sorts of activities at the conclusion of a warm up for technical-tactical training.

For the purposes of the development of rhythm/relaxation during off-seasons and *speed in certain cases:

- Speed Endurance and Special Endurance Runs- while this may seem counterintuitive at first (regarding the preparation of field sport athletes) the performance of runs from 80 out to 300meters offers a unique opportunity to think while moving relatively fast- yet not maximally fast in terms of intensity. This allows for greater forebrain activity without the expense of creating technical issues elsewhere as is often observed when a sprinter is given too much to think about (too many verbal cues often solves and creates problems simultaneously). The distance of the runs provides the coach the opportunity to make more than one verbal cue without overloading the athlete.The longer distance instinctually causes the athletes to relax more than an untrained sprinter would during a short sprint yet the distances are short enough to not cause the athlete to slow down too much. Athletes of larger bodymass would be limited to runs on the shorter distance end of the scale.
- *These runs can actually serve as a speed development stimulus for athletes of lower sprint preparation because the speed they are able to maintain over the distance may be within 10% of the speed they can generate at maximum velocity. So while speed and special endurance, in the traditional sense, will typically not be on the forebrain of most conditioning coaches- they shouldn't be that much of a stretch when one thinks of how common they are in the preparation of T&F jumpers (whose approach runs are consistent with acceleration distances found in field sports), again for the purposes of the development of rhythm.

Regarding off-season periods, any form of sprint training is open for debate yet must successfully pass cost: benefit/ risk: reward discussions.

Speed in sport, in the truest alactic sense, must be limited to the alactic period which varies according to output ability. By definition, the alactic period ceases to exist when the athlete ceases to accelerate and reaches maximum velocity. Regarding most field sport athletes this will happen between 20-40meters.

In terms of programming the training load, regardless if in the context of programme management or solely off-season physical preparation, a high/low sequence of alternating load intensity is strongly suggested. This is so because the preparations of field/court/ice sport athletes requires the development of multiple training targets and their effective management, in reference to workload versus recovery, is possible through the high/low framework.

In a High/Low system, largely popularized by Charlie Francis, any form of running that may not be recovered from in 24 hours is treated as a high intensity component (regardless of where it falls in the range of 75-100% intensity range).

For coaches with a track background, this includes starts, accelerations, maximum velocity, speed endurance, special endurance I, special endurance II, and intensive tempo. For coaches who do not have a track background, here are the runs and their associated parameters for sprinters (note that the distances associated with the time ranges are based upon the results of higher level sprinters and would thus be adjusted for most field sport athletes who will not cover as much ground in the given time):

Intensive Tempo: 75-85% intensity over various distances
Special Endurance II: <45seconds, 300-600meters
Special Endurance I: 15-45seconds, 150-300meters
Speed Endurance: 8-15seconds, 80-150meters
Alactic Speed: <8seconds, <80meters

In a high/low system one or more combinations of these runs, including starts and short accelerations, may be performed in the same session but not on consecutive days. A minimum of 48 hours would separate training days containing these medium to high intensity activities and be separated by low intensity training days in which any running would be limited to beneath the 75th percentile of intensity. *Take note technical-tactical coaches and consider the nature of consecutive training days and at what intensities you are planning the workloads.

During off-season, or pre-season programme management scenarios, the following load volume parameters for alactic speed work may be considered and were recommended by Charlie Francis:

Distance	Effort	Reps	Total Volume
<30m	Max	6-8	180-240m
50m	Max	5-6	250-300m
60m	Max	4-6	240-360m

Whenever speed work is being performed in conjunction with technical-tactical training periods, void of programme management, the conditioning coach(es) must track the approximate volumes of high-max intensity running and then consider subtracting those volumes from the accepted totals . If the average volume of high to max intensity sprints during technical-tactical trainings exceeds the accepted totals than the conditioning coach must exercise extreme caution in planning the volume, if any, of additional speed work to subsequent training days.

In the context of technical-tactical field sport training, and knowing that the vast majority of field/court sports are alactic-aerobic (only differing in proportionality), while most of the faster sprint efforts are restricted to the alactic distance, the practice activities themselves are often not honoring alactic training parameters. Incomplete recoveries and/or extended bouts of higher intensity actions are often instructed not because they are associated with the majority of field sport time:motion competition actions; but because insufficient coaching education renders technical-tactical as well as conditioning coaches under the belief that frequent lactic loading is essential to field/court sport preparation.

Assuming there is no programme management in place, if the conditioning coach swallows the red pill (see The Matrix) before the technical-tactical staff, then the conditioning coach must understand that it is important to perform the alactic sprint loading, in cautious volumes, prior to the lactic loading and on the same day. It is unlikely that a high/low sequence of field loading is being practiced by the technical-tactical staff so care must be taken regarding the conditioning coach's loading on the adjacent days of training in which it is likely that technical-tactical practices will involve more lactic loading. The reason this scenario can work, regarding the lack of high/low integrity, is because most non-track athletes have adapted to the daily technical-tactical loading of lactic or quasi-lactic efforts and in time this becomes background noise. Consequently, very conservatively dosed efforts that are of higher quality may be safely added to the equation while posing no threat.

Alternatively, during off-seasons, in which the conditioning coach is in primary control, or regarding programme management scenarios in which the programme manager is in control of the physical stress incurred by the athletes, a proportionality scheme must be put in place in reference to the dominant training modality at any given time.

If speed is determined to be of importance then speed work assumes the dominant modality role and all other training load elements must be carefully arranged around it. In this way, the high/low scheme proves highly economical as it allows for the continued performance/practice of many other load elements albeit at lessened volumes.

During competition calendars, while it may seem counterintuitive, at first, for technical-tactical loading to take a back seat to speed work, one must take a closer look at the actual proportionality, as well as contribution, scheme that shapes the biodynamic/bioenergetic structure of the sport/discipline itself. After having done so, many field sport coaches will soon realize that acceleration development and technical-tactical loading are effectively mutually dependent:

- speed of acceleration is one of the primary commonalities shared between all sports played on a field, court, or ice
- speed development necessitates mechanical optimization and intensities must not exceed

mechanical correctness

- once mechanics are in place the efforts must works towards maximal intensities separated by full recoveries
- locomotive speed is often inseparable from the execution of technical-tactical maneuvers.
- Acceleration speed will not be advanced to its potential in the presence of performing technical-tactical maneuvers.
- Technical-tactical maneuvers will not be enhanced in their efficiency if athletes are required to intensify the efforts prior to securing movement skill.

Speed training must then be separated from technical-tactical loading and technical-tactical loading must not be intensified (speed, force, etcetera...) prior to the development of movement efficiency.

Only when the two are sufficiently advanced in their own realms may they be effectively unified (ergo technical-tactical scrimmaging, small sided games, and so on). Technical-tactical loading, no different than speed work, must not be intensified prior to the development of mechanical efficiency.

Training parameters associated with sprint speed development cover intensity, volume, and frequency. They have been established over time and in relation to the training of world class athletes. In order to develop world class speed every sprinter must work to maximize their movement efficiency which then reduces mechanical stress to the body while enhancing power outputs. Through intelligently structured and individualized training schedules sprinters are able to develop these qualities while minimizing injuries.

Sprinting is a skill and at the neuromuscular level it involves some of the most highly synchronized and dynamic forms of muscle activity found in sport. The successful development of world class sprint speed involves the ability to taper and peak for competitions and, ultimately, to exhibit the highest results at the biggest competitions. The margins for error in sprinting are some of the smallest in all of sport. Reaction times, mechanics, smoothness of transitioning through race phases, and relaxation are some of the factors that, if negatively affected by the slightest decrement, can result in dramatic differences in race outcomes. This means executing the height of one's current potential at every competition and then developing this ability and executing the new found levels at the larger events- all desirably qualities for non-track athletes.

Alternatively, many team sports, due to the team dynamic and technical-tactical factors, are built upon the possibility that a player can, for example, have the game of their life in the face of injury to a non-essential limb or body segment. Not the case for the sprinter.

Technical-tactical maneuvers are movements, simple to complex, based upon decision. Neurophysiology dictates each athletes speed of processing information (sensory input) and physiological and motor qualities dictate what that athlete can do once the decision has been made.

If a coach accepts that the consistent and heightened sport skill (technical-tactical) execution is the apex of competition expectations than he/she must also accept that there is a logical sequence of events that leads toward an athlete or team's ability to demonstrate continued and reliable results. This is so because the physical aspect of executing competition maneuvers are movements built upon trainable and quantifiable motor qualities (reactive/elastic ability, agility, speed, power, strength, stamina, ...)

Sprint speed development involves the knowledge of how to develop multiple qualities for a singular purpose and competitions provide nearly no room for error.

In team sports- execution beats scheme, execution is based upon the training of measurable qualities, and the continued advancement and peaking of non-track athlete sport skill execution will be enhanced through the coaching staff's understanding of applied sprint training.

XVIII. PROGRAM EXAMPLES

The following program examples illustrate the longer term outlines that were constructed for each athlete as well as actual text overviews representative of the different stages of preparation.

The means by which sprint training may be integrated into the training load are varied. The objective is to ensure that the proportionality and contribution of and between various load elements is logical relative to the athlete's traits, where they are in relation to the competition calendar, and the structure of their competition demands.

The training program outlines were provided in order to illustrate some of the ways sprint training have been successfully integrated into the preparations of my athlete's and teams competing in various sports around the world via the high/low method. Note the interplay between the various load elements and how the loading schemes modulate over time relative to the approaching competition calendar.

The inclusion of actual bullet point text overviews, that were devised for each client, should provide more clarity to each program outline.

The outlines are taken from athletes who compete, or competed, in the following sports:

- T&F Decathlon
- T&F 100m
- Professional Canadian Football (CFL) Defensive Back
- European Team Handball
- Professional American Football (NFL) Quarterback
- Collegiate American Football- Skill Positions- University of Pittsburgh 2009
- International Rugby Sevens

T&F DECATHLETE PREPARATION

OFF-SEASON

Week	Week of:	Training
15	5-20	GPP/Tempo + Extensive Power Speed + MB + Accumulation Wts
14	5-27	GPP/Tempo + Extensive Power Speed + MB + Accumulation Wts
13	6-3	GPP/Tempo + Extensive Power Speed + MB + Accumulation Wts
12	6-10	GPP/Tempo + Extensive Power Speed + MB + Accumulation Wts
11	6-17	GPP/Hill Sprint + Jumps Up + MB + Tempo + Accumulation Wts
10	6-24	GPP/Hill Sprint + Jumps Up + MB + Tempo + Accumulation Wts
9	7-1	GPP/Hill Sprint + Jumps Up + MB + Tempo + Accumulation Wts
8	7-8	Hill Sprint + Stair Jumps + MB + Tempo + Max Strength Wts
7	7-15	Hill Sprint + Stair Jumps + MB + Tempo + Max Strength Wts
6	7-22	Flat/Hill Sprint + Stair Jumps + MB + Tempo + Max Strength Wts
5	7-29	Flat/Hill Sprint + Repeat Horizontal Hops + MB + Tempo + Deload Wts
4	8-5	Sprints on Flats + Repeat Horizontal Hops + MB + Tempo + Max Strength Wts
3	8-12	Sprints on Flats + Repeat Horizontal Hops + MB + Tempo + Max Strength Wts
2	8-19	Sprints on Flats + Repeat Vertical Hops + MB + Tempo + Max Strength Wts
1	8-26	Sprints on Flats + Repeat Vertical Hops + MB + Tempo + Deload Wts

Through discussion it was decided that no direct work for the 1500m would take place over the 15 week training period as the athlete would subsequently be partaking in a training camp with his club for a period of weeks prior to the competition calendar. The athlete requested that the program reflect more general and specialized preparatory means of training as he felt confident in his event specific technical preparation such that he would have enough time to address it during his club training period that would follow this 15 week program.

Initial Overview:

- The 1500m event is the oddball. Due to your, up to date, low tolerance for CNS stress we are going to introduce all running and power speed work at an extensive capacity
- I'm inclined to reserve the 'training' for the 1500m to tempo/tempo circuits and reserve any direct long runs (+800m) at competition speed for your club training after September
- We'll treat your September and October training with the club as your true SPP, however, because we have 15 weeks to go we will be touching on elements of SPP, from a training load intensity perspective, prior to September
- What we must determine is whether you'll more positively respond/tolerate a long to short, short to long, or combined approach to the speed work. We'll be able to get a feel for this depending on how everything progresses these first 4 weeks
- This first 4 week block of training I'm going to remove the sprint/hill sprints that you've been doing and we're only going to to tempo variations (on flats and hills), extensive power speed, and weights/throws. This will prime and prepare your anatomical structures for the work to come. You have plenty of time so this will prove to be the most intelligent approach
- I've always favored a general approach to the weights, with the exception of special strength exercises according to event. Thus, it is not my favor to include Olympic lift variations in the training. After all, every sub 9.8 sprinter, as Charlie Francis said, in history has used a general approach and the great Anatoliy Bondarchuk found that, of all

weight training exercises, the bench press showed more transfer to world class level throws than any other barbell exercise.

Weights:
- Weights follow speed. Don't get caught up in the numbers. I'm having you perform a very rudimentary program these first four weeks of primary and secondary circuits. NOTHING is to be performed anywhere close to failure. Take incomplete rests between exercises within the same circuit (less than 2minutes)
- Tune in to how you feel each and every day and select weights accordingly that give you a moderate challenge to complete the repetitions
- keep a training log so you may keep track of the weights you are using from week to week with the only directive to increase the weight, where applicable, from one week to the next
- I do not write warm up sets for the weights so do what you need to do to get ready

Explosive Medicine Ball Throws
- OHB- overhead backwards
- BLF- between the legs forwards
- Hop + Squat - you'll hop once or twice then sink into a half squat and explode out into the throw
- Rotational- similar to the release of the hammer you'll start low and release high across your body

Tempo (Hill and Flat)
- Run smooth, I don't care about times. Just run smooth and relaxed and below the 75% percentile
- On the hill, you'll perform the pressups or abs immediately after the run then walk back down the hill
- Walk around for 2-3minutes between each set of hill runs
- On the flats, you'll run on the sideline of the field, immediately perform the pressups or abs, then walk across the field about 30-50m then run back down towards the start. So you'll be walking 30-50m across the width after each set of pressups or abs. Then walk 100m between each set of runs

Extensive Power Speed
- the key here is to perform all the drills at an extensive level of intensity. focus only on rhythm and relaxation. I'm having you perform the drills over 30m; however, it should feel like you could keep going out to 100m. Smooth, smooth, smooth

Abs
- I only want you to perform spine stabilization exercises for this 4 week block. I'll email you video examples.

Overview Weeks 6-17 through 7-8:
- My exploratory interests for the first four weeks were to determine your tolerance. Based upon your feedback we'll limit the running/ground impact stress to 4 days per week. 2 speed and 2 tempo
- I'm going to reduce the distance for each power speed rep to 10-20m
- Three intensive training elements are being added in the form of hill sprints, explosive jumps up (down easy), and explosive pushups up (down easy)
- Hill sprints are self explanatory (always to be done on grass) and the explosive jumps up may be done onto any surface that challenges you (box, table, wall, stairs). For the jumps, you are to land in a squat position no deeper than parallel (in order to maintain a neutral lumbar spine) so ensure that the surface is not too high. The focus here is maximum vertical hip displacement, not to see if you can get your knees up by your ears. You are to land with balance and as quietly as possible. Step down to the floor between reps
- For the pushups up, you may do these onto boxes, benches, stacks of bumper plates, milk crates, or what ever you have available. The goal here, similar to the jumps up, is the maximum vertical displacement of your torso so, again similar to the jumps up, I want you to land no deeper than 90 degrees at the elbow and land quietly. Walk your hands down to the floor between reps.
- Please get me as much video as you can so I can have a look at how you move, particularly regarding sprinting and power speed

Weights

- As we near the end of accumulation I'm going to transition you to performing the weights based upon a 'key' session approach. This is an idea I've take from Charlie and various Russian resources
- Your primary lifts are arm extensor (presses) and leg extensor (leg press and half squat). All other lifts are secondary. Thus you will select one session each week to emphasize the arm press and another, on a different day, for the leg extensor. You have 4 sessions each week, 2 upper and 2 lower, so 1 of the 2 upper days will be emphasized for the arm extensor and 1 of the 2 lower body days will be emphasized for the leg extensor.
- The emphasis will come in the form of volume. I'll program the intensity zone; however, you will now push the volume on the 'key' session for the respective lift (arm or leg extensor).
- I'm adding a special exercise for the javelin- pull overs. Let me know how your shoulders do with these. Try them with a few different barbells and if they are not comfortable in any way then do not do them
- The new split features further consolidation of intensive stressors:

Monday Upper Body weights/arm jumps + Tempo
Tuesday Hill Sprints + Explosive Throws + Lower Body Weights/Jumps
Wednesday Bike Tempo
Thursday Same as Monday
Friday Same as Tuesday
Saturday Same as Wednesday
Sunday OFF

- If you were to select Monday as the key session for the arm extensors and Friday as the key session for the leg extensors, then Thursday and Tuesday would be particularly low volume. Again, I'm only programming the zone of intensity. The key session only applies to one lift.
- As we get deeper into this process you will see that I'm placing more and more responsibility on you. For example, I'm no longer programming the exact weight training exercises, only the regime. You have your experiences with a variety of exercises this past block to decide what suits you best on any given day. By regime, I will only write arm extensor, arm flexor, shoulders/scapula, leg/hip extensor, and back/hip extensor
- Arm extensor is any press, Arm flexor is any row or pullup, shoulders/scapula is any single joint deltoid or cuff work, leg/hip extensor is any squat, leg press, split squat, lunge, and back/hip extensor is any back extension, RDL, good morning.

Week of 7-15 Max Strength Weights Wk 2

*Your latest report indicated that everything is going very well. As a result, I want to continue with having you work off of the intensity zones for the upper body. If you are not agreeable with this then let me know and I'll program the arm extensor load in more detail.
*This week is very similar to last week with the exception of increased intensity zones on primary weights
*Movements that register high in Fv will intensify each week (when programming is sound) so even though volume may stay the same, or reduce, the intensity still goes up if you are sprinting faster, jumping farther/higher, throwing farther.

Week of 7-22 Max Strength Weights Wk 3

*Introduction of sprints on the flat
*It is imperative that you get me video of you sprinting on the flat. Make sure the video is taken from the side and the sun is to the back of the camera
*The speed comes first so even though the weights are in max strength mode you must yield to how you feel as a result of the speed work. Do not sacrifice speed sessions for weights. Decrease the intensity zone of the lower weights if need be.
*From this point forward, I only want you to perform a dedicated power speed session 2x/week. The days you perform these are up to you. They may be performed before tempo or on the bike tempo days. Obviously you are already performing some power speed during your sprint warm up but I don't want that to be programmed per se. The power speed at the end of Warm up I is just to get you ready to sprint so don't mistake that for a dedicated power speed session.

Week of 7-29 Deload Weights

*Pushup landings transition into clapping pushups
*Stair Bounds transition to horizontal hops on the flat. These are double leg hops performed consecutively without pausing
*Med Ball Hop + Throw transitions into a shot throw (see my youtube channel under explosive med ball)
*I'm going to start increasing the length of some of the tempo reps as well as the overall volume, very gradually, in order to prepare you for special endurance runs. Still treat these like regular tempo (smooth and relaxed). These will not interfere with your speed work as long as you keep the intensity below 75% so DO NOT push the intensity (speed) of the tempo. The way to increase the challenge of tempo is NOT to increase the speed of the runs; but rather, to decrease the rest intervals between each run
*Introduction of special endurance (this is for your 400m training)
*Tuesday will be speed days and Friday will be special endurance (but you'll still do short speed on Friday before the special endurance)
*Since I've started you on short to long I'm going to have you perform split runs for the special endurance. These will be back to back 60m reps performed by using an intensity limit.
*20m intensity limit. The total length of the sprint is 60m but you will only accelerate to 20m then maintain the remaining 40m. Set cones up at the 20m mark and just go into cruise control (don't decelerate and don't accelerate, just maintain) to the 60m mark. This intensity limit will gradually increase over the weeks until you are performing the full 60m as sprint.

Week of 8-12

- The number of running sessions have been further reduced to 2x/week- sprints only
- Continue to perform all sprints and jumps on grass
- All tempo work is to be performed in the pool or on the bike. I don't want to have you perform more power speed for aerobic development because of the ground impacts so we'll limit the ground impacts to sprints and jumps and the already existing power speed unless you feel that you would like to eliminate the existing power speed
- You already know what to do for bike tempo
- For pool tempo you will perform 2-3 sets of 10 in which you'll perform high knees in place in the shallow end of the pool for 20seconds. Take 20-30sec rest between sets and wait to perform your press ups and abs until you complete each set. Perform 5 rounds of (press ups and abs) between each set of 10 high knees in the pool
- In order to increase the amount of dorsi flexion at the ankle you can generate you may attempt the following methods after you have already heated up the area with some local warm up:
    - get into the position of a lunge/hip flexor stretch with your front foot elevated on a box/bench approximately 30cm high. Begin to lean/lunge forward onto the elevated foot and continue forward as far as possible as long as you keep the heel in contact with the box/bench. This places a stretch on the achilles/calf. You may also add a stretch band to the mix by placing the band around the ankle and securing it at floor level behind you.
    - Perform self massage to the junction of the achilles/calf in the stretched position of ankle dorsi flexion
    - Perform self PNF for the achilles/calf by using your bodyweight. Get into position as if you are going to do heel/calf raises with the balls of your feet elevated on a step/box/bench/edge of a platform. Descend into the stretched position and hold for 3-5 seconds then relieve the stretch by taking the foot off the surface. Repeat this for 5-6 repetitions.
    - Visit a soft tissue specialist. Graston is a technique that may be beneficial in this instance
- Clapping pushups are replaced with rebound box pushups (see my youtube channel)
- I'm refraining from introducing single leg bound/jump exercises in favor of taking it easy on your lower legs. Let's get your lower legs restored first

T&F 100M SPRINTER

Month	Week of:	Training Block	Sprint Type	Start Type	Distance Per Rep	Jumps Type	Med Ball Weekly	Weights	Low Int MB Abs High Day	Low Day
Sep	5th	Transition	Sled-Drills	High	30m	Up into Pit	60-70	Accum	300	600
	12th		Sled-Drills	High	30m	Up into Pit	70-80	Accum	300	600
	19th		Sled-Drills	High	30m	Up into Pit	80-90	Accum	350	700
	26th		Sled-Drills	High	30m	Up into Pit	90-100	Deload	400	800
Oct	3rd	GPP	Sled	High	10-30m	Up + Off	120	Accum	500	1000
	10th		Sled	High	40m	Up + Off	90	Accum	550	1100
	17th		Sled	High	40m	Up + Off	60	Accum	600	1200
	24th		Sled	High	40m	Up + Up + Off	60	Accum	650	1300
	31st		Flats	PU/High	10-60m	Up + Up + Off	60	Accum	700	1400
Nov	7th		Flats	PU/High	10-60m	Up + Up + Off	60	MxS	700	1400
	14th		Flats	PU/High	10-60m	Hurdle Hops	60	MxS	500	1000
	21st	SPP1	Flats	PU/High	10-60m	Hurdle Hops	60	MxS	400	800
	28th		Flats	PU/High	10-60m	Hurdle Hops	60	Deload	800	1600
Dec	5th		Flats	PU/High	10-60m	Drop + Hurdle	60	MxS	800	1600
	12th		Flats	Block/High	10-60m	Drop + Hurdle	60	MxS	600	1200
	19th		Flats	Block/High	10-60m	Drop + Hurdle	60	MxS	500	1000
	26th		Flats	Block/High	10-60m	Hurdle	60	Deload		

This European athlete and I had been working together for three years prior to the commencement of this program. He had recently made the shift from training as a discus thrower to a 100m sprinter.

You will notice the GIRD rehab, this reflects a previously diagnosed condition.

Transition Block Overview Excerpt:

- The outline, based upon Charlie's work, is to be used as a guide; nothing more and nothing less. In actuality, with respect to each training day, I am providing you with ranges, as opposed to set instructions for the majority of your training. This is inspired from Dan Pfaff and based upon the logic that it is wise for you to have a degree of ownership over the work that is completed each day. The low ends of the range are created based upon what I think are required for you to experience the targeted adaptations while the upper ends of the range exist for you to keep going if you feel really good.

- Changes are likely to occur once we have the January competition schedule

Speed Work
- Even though you've been sprinting over the last block, I'm transitioning you to the sled performing intensive tempo runs to prepare you for sled sprints in October. This will allow us to quickly take you to 30m.
- I could have obviously had you perform intensive tempo without the sled; however, I decided to go with the sled to prepare your muscles for it when the faster sprints roll around
- You'll run these at what feels like a 75-85% effort and keep the rests short/incomplete

GPP Block Overview Excerpt:
- Restart Accumulation, Introduce Alactic Sled Sprints on GRASS, Re-introduce extensive tempo- no sled (ONLY on GRASS), Incorporate Arm Pulls every session, Eliminate High Pulls and Front Squats
- It is CRITICAL that you do not go too fast on the tempo as it is now extensive. It can be as slow as a jog but no faster than 75%. Use the calisthenics that you'll perform after each run and the rest intervals to challenge yourself- NOT the speed of the runs themselves. I think it would be wise for you to begin this week of tempo moving in the 50% range and gradually increase towards 75%, assuming you feel good, over the weeks.
- Let's see how you like doing tempo after the weights and feel free to do more or less warm up before and after weights to get ready for each

- All Jumps are up onto a box and off into the high jump pit- up and off = 1 rep, squats and chest presses are now to be semi-auto regulated by you according to the modified chart I'm sending to you- I assign the intensity zone and you select the volume, arm pulls are any type of row you want to do
- Remember that sprinting IS an arm pulling activity so it is not necessary that you perform an excessive amount of arm pulling volume with weights. For this reason, I believe that the more speed work you do the more your shoulders will adjust into more optimal alignment
- Utilize incomplete recoveries this week only on the sled sprints, recoveries for subsequent weeks are listed at the top of each week's plan
- Remember, weights follow speed so adjust as needed following the speed sessions

Overview Excerpt Going into SPP:

- Deep tissue options on day 1, 2, and 5 as well
- As soon as you receive your massage table I want you to have pre-training massage (light/slapping/stimulatory/exploratory) performed EVERY day, with the most important days being the speed days and I want post-training massages (light/flushing) after every speed session as well
- considering this weekly taxonomy, we must ensure that we address starts/short speed and max V because we don't need to introduce speed endurance until SPP 2
- I do believe that it will be wise to address special endurance in the form of repeat 60m in order to prepare you for multiple heat indoor competitions
- In so doing, we will utilize intensity limits, which we've already used, as far as limiting the distance over which you accelerate prior to maintaining for the remainder of the 60m.
- Day 3 we will address starts and short speed (<30m) and Day 6 we'll include more starts and short speed as well as special endurance 60m repeats with intensity limits that will begin with 20m and finalize with you covering the full 60m prior to beginning the taper for your first indoor meet
- the total volume of starts/short speed will be higher on Day 3 and lower on day 6 in order to leave more available volume for the special endurance 60m work on day 6
- you already have a fantastic sense of your readiness for throws/jumps/weights so we'll continue with me providing guidelines and you decide what is useful any given day
- You are free to disperse the weight training over the course of the week because you only have 2 speed days to recover from. Bench and upper body can be done on any day and here are some squat training day options that are compatible with the new split:
    - Day 1 and Day 3
    - Day 1 and Day 4
    - Day 3 and Day 6
    - Day 3 and Day 7
    - Day 4 and Day 6
    - Day 4 and Day 7
- the most important factor is that you are maximizing your readiness for speed days so feel free to experiment with a few in order that we may determine which is the most optimal
- I want to reinforce my instruction that ALL speed work be performed smoothly and sub-maximal. Intensification will occur naturally as time moves forward so DO NOT push the intensity in terms of effort. Just move relaxed over the given distance
- We'll wait to introduce block starts until about 4 weeks prior to the first meet. Until then, I want you to practice all starts by using various pushup starts (bottom position and top position of the pushup). Don't concern yourself with any technicalities, just scramble up and out and pump your arms
- We'll use tempo circuits from Charlie to keep things from becoming monotonous. I'm going to list the full circuits; however, you can feel free to begin this week by reducing the volume of each session if you don't feel that you're up to it from the get go

PROFESSIONAL CANADIAN FOOTBALL DEFENSIVE BACK

Week of:	Week	Block	Sprints	Weights	Jumps	Pushups	Throws	Tempo
3 Dec	26	1	Power Speed 10m	Accumulation	Roll/5m, Rhythmic Rebound 10sec/25cm	Decline Rhythmic Clap 10sec	Rebound Close	Running A 30m
10 Dec	25		Power Speed 15m	Accumulation	Roll/10m, Rhythmic Rebound 10sec/30cm	Decline Rhythmic Clap 15sec	Rebound 5m	Running A 40m
17 Dec	24		Power Speed 20m	Accumulation	Roll/15m, Rhythmic Rebound 10sec/35cm	Decline Rhythmic Clap 20sec	Rebound 5m	Running A 50m
24 Dec	23	2	Alactic Capacity	Accumulation	Box Jump Up	Up Only	OHB/BLF/Divex10ea	60mx10
31 Dec	22		Alactic Capacity	Accumulation	Box Jump Up	Up Only	OHB/BLF/Divex10ea	60mx10
7 Jan	21		Alactic Power	Max Strength	Box Jump Up	Up Only	OHB/BLF/Divex10ea	60mx2x6
14 Jan	20		Alactic Power	Max Strength	Box Jump Up&Off	Down	OHB/BLF/Divex8ea	60mx2x6
21 Jan	19	3	Alactic Power	Max Strength	Box Jump Up&Off	Down	OHB/BLF/Divex8ea	60mx2x8
28 Jan	18		Alactic Power	Deload	Box Jump Up&Off	Down	OHB/BLF/Divex8ea	60mx2x8
4 Feb	17		Alactic Power	Max Strength	Stair Jumps	Rebound	OHB/BLF/Divex6ea	60mx2x10
11 Feb	16		Alactic Power	Max Strength	Stair Jumps	Rebound	OHB/BLF/Divex6ea	60mx2x10
18 Feb	15	4	Alactic Power	Max Strength	Stair Jumps	Rebound	OHB/BLF/Divex6ea	60mx2x10
25 Feb	14		Alactic Capacity	Accumulation	Box Jump Up&Off	Up Only	OHB/BLF/Divex10ea	60mx3x8
4 Mar	13		Alactic Capacity	Accumulation	Box Jump Up&Off	Up Only	OHB/BLF/Divex10ea	60mx3x8
11 Mar	12		Alactic Capacity	Accumulation	Box Jump Up&Off	Up Only	OHB/BLF/Divex9ea	60mx4x7
18 Mar	11	5	Alactic Capacity	Accumulation	Box Jump Up&Off	Up Only	OHB/BLF/Divex8ea	60mx4x7
25 Mar	10		Alactic Power	Max Strength	Stair Jumps	Down	OHB/BLF/Divex8ea	60mx4x8
1 Apr	9		Alactic Power	Max Strength	Stair Jumps	Down	OHB/BLF/Divex7ea	60mx4x8
8 Apr	8		Alactic Power	Max Strength	Stair Jumps	Down	OHB/BLF/Divex7ea	60mx4x9
15 Apr	7	6	Alactic Power	Deload	Hurdle Hops	Rebound	OHB/BLF/Divex6ea	60mx4x9
22 Apr	6		Alactic Power	Max Strength	Hurdle Hops	Rebound	OHB/BLF/Divex6ea	60mx4x10
29 Apr	5		Alactic Power	Max Strength	Hurdle Hops	Rebound	OHB/BLF/Divex5ea	60mx4x10
6 May	4		Alactic Power	Max Strength	Hurdle Hops	Rebound	OHB/BLF/Divex5ea	60mx4x10
13 May	3	7	Alactic Capacity	Maintenance	Repeat Hops	Clapping	OHB/BLF/Divex10ea	60mx4x10
20 May	2		Alactic Capacity	Maintenance	Repeat Hops	Clapping	OHB/BLF/Divex8ea	60mx4x10
27 May	1		Alactic Capacity	Maintenance	Repeat Hops	Clapping	OHB/BLF/Divex6ea	60mx4x10

The logistics of the CFL provide for a substantial off-season. This athlete plays in the defensive backfield and was already in possession of tremendous speed/power/strength qualities prior to enlisting my distance coaching services. The emphasis of his training was the global advancement of relevant qualities, particularly speed/explosiveness and enhanced positional specific movement efficiency, without any particular priority being placed on his general strength development. As described earlier in this manual, however, a bi-product of his neuromuscular demanding speed/power and position specific work resulted in even more gains in general strength as realized in the bench press and squat.

CFL Initial Overview Excerpt:

- You will see from the outline that each training element goes through phases of intensification and method of execution.
- All transitions are smooth edged
- The outline is very flexible and subject to numerous modifications depending upon many variables
- I always write sets x reps so 10x2 = 10sets of 2reps, and in the case of series I write series x sets x reps so 2 x (3x5)= 2 series of 3sets x 5reps
- You are to send me as much video as possible in order to ensure that you are executing mechanical efficiency on all movements no matter how insignificant you think they may be
- Most important are the mechanical execution of the CNS intensive training components; however, even the way you perform pushups is important because every inefficiency comes at a price
- Always film sprints, power speed, throws, and jumps from the side and try to position the light source behind the camera
- You'll see how block 1 and 7 are 3 weeks in length. This is only for illustration purposes. I will be sending you 4weeks of training at a time even though there will be some overlap regarding the actual block
- Notice the relationship between primary weights and auxiliary weights: the accumulation of primary weights moves from higher volume/lesser intensity to lower volume/higher intensity and the auxiliary weights do just the opposite by providing the opportunity for greater loads early/at lesser volumes and move to higher volumes/that necessitate lesser loads and this is done in order to provide the requisite stimuli at the appropriate time
- Always review my youtube page for examples of movements and then perform searches on youtube if need be then verify with me that a movement is correct by sending me a link or what have you
- Regarding block 1, the only exercise descriptions you should need are for one of the jump variations (rhythmic rebounds) and the pushup variation (decline rhythmic clapping pushups)
- Rhythmic Rebound Jumps- these are a vertical version of the rolling hops (which you can see on my youtube channel). Jump on and off a surface consistent with the heights I've written and focus on deep knee bend counter movements on the box/bench/bumpers as well as on the ground. You should be very quiet on all contacts. I'll need to see video to ensure that he's doing these as I wish.
- Decline Rhythmic Clapping Pushup- these are essentially the jumping version for the arms. Use an elevated surface for your hands to reduce the percentage of bodyweight that you have to overcome. I suggest a bench or even higher. Elbow bends and contact sound must be very similar to the rhythmic jumps, large amplitude bends and quiet contacts.
- Neither the jumps or the pushups are to be performed explosively, while the movements are elastic, they are rather slow in nature and you'll really feel them in the muscles
- Your level of physical preparation, as indicated on the questionnaire, is very good (speed, power, strength) thus I want to be clear in stating that this training is not designed to chase numbers for their own sake; but to improve the most relevant physical and technical preparatory qualities as we will begin to address technical aspects in the second block
- As for your interest in training alone, I am the same way. I began my formal training in the late 80s and since then there may have only been one year, in total, when I had partners. I've been training for over twenty years and I've never missed a week of training. I don't ask athletes to do anything that I haven't already done.
- Lastly, training is a living breathing thing and what I program is highly flexible. These programs are only guidelines and it is your call as to whether you will either reduce or eliminate any particular aspect of the workload on any given day based upon how you feel. Do not fall into the trap of feeling obligated to complete what is written. We have to learn together in terms of your tolerance for CNS stress and your adaptation rates

CFL Weeks 14,13,12,11 Overview

- While we haven't been acutely monitoring all elements (times/distances/heights) your preparation has been, in my view, progressing well
- Now that you have completed a 7 week intensification scheme we will drop to another accumulation phase that will allow your system to stabilize to the new found gains via the reduction in intensity yet still allow for continued development through enhanced work capacity in nearly all elements
- In terms of load volume and intensity, all training elements will transition back to the logical proportionality

scheme in which greater volume/lesser intensity gradually shifts in proportionality back to lesser volume/greater intensity (even greater than before). Hence 1 step back and 2 steps forward

- Performing the sprints in a capacity environment, via decreased rest intervals to regulate intensity, is compatible with the accumulation weights. An oversimplification would be to state that accumulation phases stimulate morphology while intensification phases transmute the morphological gains into advanced neuromuscular efficiency

- The tempo work is the one element that is, and has been, progressing linearly, in terms of volume, and that is because the intensity is static/sub-max. The distances remain short in order to adjust to the indoor area. One modification, however, is in the method of execution.

- I'm going to initiate you having the option to perform multi-directional tempo work, while still continuing with the linear runs. Alternate a linear run with a run that involves more than one way of traveling down field (side shuffling, cross over running, carioca, back pedal, easy S shaped swerves during back pedal, sub-max speed turns, and so on). In this way, you will slow down the pace a bit on the multi-directional movement because of the greater muscular efforts required to move in those ways (again the greater muscular demand is consistent with accumulation). Also, you'll only cover 10-20meters using any one of those moves then run regular for another 10-20 then switch again. So one rep over 60meters might look like this:

- 10meters linear run
- 10meters side shuffle facing right
- 10meters linear run
- 10meters back pedal
- 10meters linear run
- 10meters side shuffle facing left

Or, 20m back pedal, 20m run normal, 20m back pedal. There are a multitude of combinations so have fun with it. The rational is that we are beginning to address the oxidative capacity in the muscles of the legs more specifically to how they function during a game

The whole time you are moving down field/or down the track in your case, you're just changing your method of travel on the way to the finish

- As for your strength improvements. I conservatively based your initial percentages off of 325 and 450. Your 315x8 and 485x5 have clearly smashed those reference points; however, I believe in bleeding the well until it is almost dry. I'm going to leave the squat training to sets x reps and continue to have you select load based upon readiness (because weights follow speed). The bench reference, however, will be adjusted, to 350 (even though I believe you certainly have 370-380 in you right now)

- Notice how some of the auxiliary work will drop in volume to allow for heavier loads to supplement the lighter loads being lifted on the primary lifts

- Since the bench variation load is very moderate in intensity, albeit higher than last accumulation block, I really want you to kick ass on the dumbbell press variants as they are your only pressing opportunity to maximally exert in a tonic sense (you have the pushups up to exert in a phasic regime/explosive). While the reps per set is increasing on those from week to week, I still want you to view the exercise as the one to strain on

- *One exception to the dumbbell press rule, on Fridays, if you feel really good working up on the bench, you have the option to scrap what I wrote in favor of performing 1 max set of repetitions with the working weight. If you opt to do that then you will perform the set of max reps then rest 5-6minutes before moving on to the explosive pushups. Keep in mind that we are generating more fatigue this accumulation cycle because the overall intensity is higher, in a more compressed period, than the first accumulation cycle so the goal is the cumulative result once you re-intensify

- Be prepared for some soreness as you transition back into the capacity sprints as well as higher volume squats. As a result, maximize your recovery methods

- For the alactic capacity sprints we'll have you add more variety to your starts. Mix it up between bottom pushup starts (body on the ground), top pushup starts arms extended, bottom pushup starts lying 90 degrees sideways relative to the finish line, bottom pushup starts lying 180 degrees opposite the finish line, starting kneeling on one knee facing forward, starting on one knee 90 degrees sideways relative to the finish line, and any variety of standing starts (facing forward, side ways, backwards, back pedal than break forwards, etcetera...) In the case of lateral and backward starts make sure you perform an even amount of right and left turns

- Two power speed additions, alternate leg lateral/diagonal hops and W patterns (back pedal 5m on a diagonal then break downhill on a diagonal, back pedal 5, break downhill 5m all at a relaxed power speed pace). You should be more than familiar with the W drill and the alternate leg lateral/diagonal hops are illustrated in the power speed playlist on my youtube site

CFL Weeks 10-4 Overview Excerpt

Primary Modifications

Power Speed- I will continue to add positional movements to the power speed in order to provide you with the opportunity to hone the specific movement efficiency at a very low cost. In addition to the W drills, we will add weaving back pedal (easy S shape weaves), and the speed turn, all performed sub-max just like you've been doing the W drill. In addition, similar to the 5-10-5 drill I want you to perform a 5-5-5 drill in a power speed context just like the position drills and all other drills (rhythm, relaxation, fluidity, timing, and so on). The reps for all of this does not matter. The point is exposure and movement enhancement so continue to do what you feel are useful amounts each session

Sprints- we transition back to alactic power which means higher intensities. Continue to emphasize relaxation (never forcing it) and continue to utilize the various start positions at your discretion

EFE (easy/fast/easy) you'll perform 20m easy + 20m fast + 20m easy. The key is very smooth and nearly unnoticeable transitions between each 20m segment. Your only concern is to increase the intensity/amplitude of your arm action when entering the 20m fast segment as this will be enough to raise your hip height and subsequent speed. You'll always initiate these from a standing/falling start. The acceleration should be very smooth and gradual during the first 20m then pick up the arm action for the 20m fast section, the drop the arm action down to the first 20m level of intensity and hold through the finish. If you were to assign intensities to each segment it might look like 85-90 + 90-95 + 85-90

60m with intensity limits- you'll cover 60m in total, however, you'll only accelerate over the distance which I indicate. There is great skill with this type of drill, as there is for the EFE, in that your objective is to accelerate to the written mark then hold whatever speed you've generated up to that point for the remainder of the 60m distance. You'll perform the same intensity limit for 2 weeks in a row and I'm starting you at a 20m limit. So set a cone up at 20m and another at 60m. Accelerate to the 20 then maintain to the 60. Then as I progress you, you will follow the same procedure for 30 +30, 40 + 20, then the full 60. As always, maintain relaxation throughout and NEVER force it. Start these from a standing or falling position as well

With the addition of the 60m distances there can be the tendency to drop the hammer...DON'T. I want you to continue with completely relaxed running

Jumps- the up and offs now transition back to the repeated stair jumps

Pushups- transition to down only. You'll start on top of what ever you are using for an elevated surface, explode up as high as you can off the box/bench and then land on a mat, not a hard floor). The objective is to rapidly decelerate the landing so that you finish in the halfway down position (elbows at approximately 90degrees) and hold that position for a 1count before you relax and climb your hands back on top of the box/bench. Force absorption is the objective of this method of execution.

Squats- now that we're back into intensification we'll revert back to the instruction where you only push the weights on one of the sessions and you are to rearrange the weekly order based upon which type of squat you feel like intensifying that week. If you feel like cranking it up on session 1 then you are to back off on sessions 2 and 3, and so on.

CFL Week of 5-13, Begin Final Block, Alactic Capacity, Strength Maintenance, Clapping Pushups, Repeat Hops

Positional Drills, explosive med ball throws, clapping pushups, and hops are now integrated into the Alactic capacity
Think of the Alactic Capacity somewhere between the intensities of Intensive Tempo and what I've previously instructed for Alactic Capacity- so between 80-90% intensity

EUROPEAN TEAM HANDBALL

Week	Week of	Sprints	Jumps	Throws	Pushups	Weights	Tempo per session
17	1 April	Extended Power Speed	DL Rhythmic Rebound	Wall Rebound Close	Decline Rhythmic Rebound	Strength Aerobic	1000m total
16	8 April	Extended Power Speed	DL Rhythmic Rebound	Wall Rebound Close	Decline Rhythmic Rebound	Strength Aerobic	1000m total
15	15 April	Extended Power Speed	DL Rhythmic Rebound	Wall Rebound Close	Decline Rhythmic Rebound	Strength Aerobic	1000m total
14	22 April	Sled 10/20/30	SL Rhythmic Rebound	1 Bounce Wall Rebound	Decline Clap Rhythmic Rebound	Accumulation	1400m total
13	29 April	Sled 30	SL Rhythmic Rebound	1 Bounce Wall Rebound	Decline Clap Rhythmic Rebound	Accumulation	1800m total
12	6 May	Sled 30	SL Rhythmic Rebound	1 Bounce Wall Rebound	Decline Clap Rhythmic Rebound	Accumulation	1800m total
11	13 May	Sled 30	SL Box Approach	Overhead Forward	Up Only	Accumulation	2200m total
10	20 May	Sled/No Sled	SL Box Approach	Overhead Forward	Up Only	Accumulation	2600m total
9	27 May	Sled/No Sled	SL Box Approach	Overhead Forward	Up Only	Max Strength	3000m total
8	3 June	Starts/30s	SL Up + Off	Partner Rebound Drop	Landing	Max Strength	3000m total
7	10 June	Starts/30s	SL Up + Off	Partner Rebound Drop	Landing	Max Strength	3000m total
6	17 June	Starts/30s	SL Up + Off	Partner Rebound Drop	Landing	Deload	3000m total
5	24 June	Starts/30s/Agility	SL Depth	Partner Drop Throw	Rebound	Max Strength	3000m total
4	1 July	Starts/30s/Agility	SL Depth	Partner Drop Throw	Rebound	Max Strength	3000m total
3	8 July	Starts/30s/Agility	SL Depth	Partner Drop Throw	Rebound	Max Strength	3000m total
2	15 July	Capacity	Competition SL Approach Throw		Clapping	Maintenance	2500m total
1	22 July	Capacity	Competition SL Approach Throw		Clapping	Maintenance	2000m total

This athlete contacted me having already been attempting to manage some minor pathology specific to his throwing shoulder (not an uncommon circumstance to overhead throwing athletes). The bulk of this 17 week period was unaffected from any other acting physical stress.

Initial Overview:

The programming has been constructed based upon written as well as self-executed time: motion analysis of the team handball

Primary training components:
- Sprints- I will not have you sprint until week 14. Until then, you will perform modified power speed drills in an extensive manner (longer distances) in order to extensively exercise the sprint muscle groups and quasi-motor behavior in a way that is more muscularly, and less neuromuscularly, taxing while being less structurally taxing than the sprints. Your objective while performing these extended power speed drills is rhythm and relaxation. These are the drills I want you to perform, in any order you wish, and all of them may be found on my youtube site:
  - Bum kicks
  - A Skips
  - Running A (High Knees)
  - Low Hip position lateral shuffle
  - Backward Run
  - Stiff Leg Dolly/Straight Leg Bound
  - Double Leg Zig Zag Hop
- Jumps- I will begin you with double leg (DL) rhythmic rebounds. These are an extensive form of reactive/elastic as well as muscular exercise to the jumping muscles. Note the videos of some of my athletes doing these on my youtube site
- Throws: from a specialized standpoint (which is what you see illustrated in the outline) the type and method of

execution of the throws will become more closely related to the dynamics of the competition throw as time moves forward. You will begin with wall rebounds standing as close to the wall as possible with the objective of maintaining a rigid structure so that the rebounds are small in amplitude and higher in frequency. You will perform a variety of throws in this way, overhead forward, chest, lateral with straight arms, and between the legs forward (see my youtube channel)

- Pushups- decline rhythmic rebounds, these are similar to the arm version of the rhythmic rebound jumps. In this case, your hands will be elevated on a box or bench with your feet on the floor (hence the decline position) as this will lessen the ground impact force as well as reduce the anti-gravitational stress. You will perform reactive/elastic pushups in which you will pushup just forcefully enough to separate your hands from the box/bench. The separation generates greater stretch shortening action upon take-off as well as landing; however, the over all objective is the continuous performance of this smooth movement. See videos on my youtube site
- Primary Weights- (squats/bench presses) we will being with Verkhoshansky's strength aerobic method in which the aerobic machinery is the primary bioenergetic source used for the work; yet the muscular effect is strength development. You'll use loads which allow you to perform the sets with slow overcoming and yielding action (about 3seconds per cycle) for set durations ranging between 1 and 2 minutes (so 20-40 reps at 3seconds per rep). These will burn like hell in the muscles and get you breathing pretty good. If I do not write the amount of weight on any exercise then it is up to you to select a weight that is challenging for the written time or repetitions
- Tempo- we will gradually build you up in volume to the amounts listed and your movement will not be limited to linear runs. You may vary the way in which you move; however, you will always move down field. So if you are moving laterally (low shuffle, high shuffle, lateral run, carioca) or backward (back pedal, backward run) you will do so for a segment of the run (10-30meters) then transition to another movement drill and so on until you reach the finish. You can break up the runs, into segments of different movements, any way you wish. Alternate a linear run with a multi-directional run. Alternate 10-20 pushups and 30-50 abs after each run
- If I do not list recovery times between sets or exercises than it is arbitrary and up to you to decide to go when ready
- All training components are extensive to begin with, so I will disperse the loading across all training days just to spread it around. This will remain as is through week 13.

The split through week 15 will be as follows:
- Monday/Wednesday/Friday- Med Ball + Rhythmic Rebound Jumps + Lower Body Weights + Tempo
- Tuesday/Thursday/Saturday- Extensive Power Speed + Rhythmic Rebound Pushups + Upper Body Weights

Notes- Week of June 3

- Thursday sprints- these will now be performed without the sled which means greater intensity so I'm going to limit the distance of the reps to 10meters just to work on explosive starts. I want you to initiate these a variety of ways- standing start with legs staggered, falling start, lying start (forwards as well as sideways) kneeling start in which you will vary facing forward as well as lateral relative to the running direction. On a lateral kneeling start if you are facing to the right you will be on your left knee and if you are facing to the left you will be on your right knee (this allows you to push off with the rearward leg)
- Lateral/multi-directional power speed- we have three training weeks until agility work will be executed at a high intensity so we will now integrate the movements at sub-max, relaxed, fluid intensity just like power speed drills in your warm ups. This will not be programmed work. I want you to perform some lateral/multi-directional work as a means of preparation for what is coming. Keep the drills limited to 3-6 seconds of movement, focus on relaxed and fluid movement, and let's go with lateral shuffles (without crossing the legs over), lateral run- plant- and come back (similar to a 5-10-5 drill in American football but you can limit it to 5meters-5meters-5meters), and some back pedals, plant, and move forward
- Max strength squat- pick only one squat day to work up to max weights and limit the other two to sub-max effort
- Single leg box jump up and off- you'll perform the single leg box jump up then explode again up and off into the pit. I'll also maintain a retention volume of double leg jumps up and off into the pit as well
- Partner rebound drops- https://www.youtube.com/watch?v=YsNdwM-XtDM&list=PLDC93B02665E40349&index=3
- *However you will only catch the ball and not throw it for these next 3 weeks so you will only work on the absorption of force. Notice the rapid stretch reflex resultant of catching the falling ball. I'm not going to be specific with the weight of the ball; so make your selection based upon feel. I'd say you'll use between 5-8kg
- Pushup landings- https://www.youtube.com/watch?v=JW4YCalYSmU&list=PLF2FDD527FC318510&index=1

- you'll start on top of the boxes/benches and perform an explosive pushup up and off (I want you to explode up higher than I do in the video because I didn't have a padded mat to land on) and then land on a padded mat. I want you to finish the landing in the position of 90 degree elbow bend so it will be a rapid deceleration into that position. You will hold that position of 90 degree elbow bend for a 1 second count before you reset.
- Auxiliary lower body hip/knee extensor 2 and back/hip extensor 2 are now optional to perform or not. As the speed intensifies on the flat the legs automatically receive that much more stimulation so it is your choice whether to continue to perform that stage of the auxiliary weights

Modifications: Week of June 24

- Partner rebound drop is now the rebound drop throw in which you will launch the ball as shown in the video link. You will now select the weight of the ball based upon speed of execution as this is what will determine the transference to the competition throw
- Pushup landings now transition to continuous rebounds. Start on top of the box/benches pushup up and off, rebound of the padded mat and continue
- Jumps up and off are now depth jumps. For both versions I want you to select the drop height based upon your ability to be reactive off the ground.
- Agility on Thursday- the agility work now becomes intensive and you should be fine considering the 3 prior weeks of sub-max work

Week of July 1– Mon/Wed/Fri- Max Strength

*Bench, since you worked up to a 10RM last week we will have you work to the 5RM this week
*Overload loading will become re-proportioned week to week to allow for intensification of primary elements

Week of July 1 – Tue/Thu/Sat- Max Strength

*Squats- pick one squat day and work up to a 5RM and on the other two squat days perform sub-max 2-5 sets of 3-6 reps with 55-65%

Week of July 8 – Tue/Thu/Sat- Max Strength

*Squats- pick one squat day and work up to a 3RM and on the other two squat days perform sub-max 2-5 sets of 3-6 reps with 55-65%

Week of July 15 Alactic Capacity- Reformatted Training Week

- Nomenclature for alactic capacity: series x [sets x (reps)] so 3 x [3 x (3 clapping pushups + 5-5 lateral shuffle + Competition throw)] means that you'll perform the sequence of movements continuously, moving with maximum efficiency/fluidity from one to the next until you complete the competition throw then rest 40-60 sec and repeat two more times for a total of 3 sets, Then you will rest 3-5 minutes before you perform the next series, and so on until you compete all 3 series of 3 sets for that drill. Once you have completed all series for that drill you will rest 5-6 minutes before you go to the next drill
- You'll notice some variations to the 5-5-5 lateral drills in which I have introduced both longer as well as shorter versions
- You'll have the handball on the floor next to you when you perform the clapping pushups then as soon as you finish the pushups you'll grab the ball and proceed through the sequence of movements
- As I stated, the key for these drills is to focus on executing each movement with maximum efficiency/fluidity. I want you to attack each movement as well as your transition time between movements with a sense of urgency yet maintain fluidity and optimal mechanics throughout. Think of it as the sport technical-biomotor equivalent of what

we're looking for in your sprint form- maximal output with maximal relaxation
- You'll notice the tempo volume decrease to allow for the increase in volume of alactic capacity work (which possesses its own increased aerobic demand)

NFL QUARTERBACK

Week Of	Week	Speed	Split	Jumps	Primary Lower Wts	Primary Upper Wts	SPP Wts	Throws	Tempo/session
02/06/12	1	Hill	Up-Lo	Hill Repeats	Belt Squat/GHR DL	Wt Pushup/Wt Inv Row	OHF	OHB/BLF/Rot/Snap	960
02/13/12	2	Hill	Up-Lo	Hill Repeats	Belt Squat/GHR DL	Wt Pushup/Wt Inv Row	OHF	OHB/BLF/Rot/Snap	1280
02/20/12	3	Hill	Lo-Up	Hill Repeats	Belt Squat/GHR DL	Wt Pushup/Wt Inv Row	OHF	OHB/BLF/Rot/Snap	1600
02/27/12	4	Hill	Lo-Up	Hill Repeats	SSB Box Squat/45 DL	DB Presses	Pullover	OHB/BLF/Rot	1760
03/05/12	5	Hill/Flat/Hill	Total-Aux	Flat Repeats	SSB Box Squat/45 DL	DB Presses	Pullover	OHB/BLF/Rot	1760
03/12/12	6	Flat/Hill/Flat	Total-Aux	Flat Repeats	SSB Box Squat/45 DL	DB Presses	Pullover	OHB/BLF/Rot	1760
03/19/12	7	Flat	Total-Aux	Flat Repeats	SSB Squat/RDL	DB Presses	Drop Throw	OHB/Rot	1760
03/26/12	8	Flat	Total-Aux	Hurdle Repeats	SSB Squat/RDL	DB Presses	Drop Throw	OHB/Rot	1760
04/02/12	9	Flat	Total-Aux	Hurdle Repeats	SSB Squat/RDL	DB Presses	Drop Throw	OHB/Rot	1760
04/09/12	10	Flat	Total-Aux	Hurdle Repeats	SSB Squat/RDL	DB Presses	Drop Throw	OHB/Rot	1760

This athlete secured a one year contract with a team in the NFC east during our 10 weeks of working together. I was working with this athlete in person between 4 and 6 days a week. While he had no other physical stressors competing for his attention he did have somewhat of a busy travel schedule due to sponsorships and so on. He was already a journeyman NFL veteran having been in the league since 2007 and started over 30 games. As a collegiate athlete he was the starting quarterback for a major Pac 10 program and the second highest rated quarterback in his draft class according to certain analysts.

The team he signed with would require that he perform certain Olympic lift variations upon his arrival. This was reflected in our preparation; yet only at a technical level.

COLLEGIATE AMERICAN FOOTBALL

University of Pittsburgh 2009 Calendar

- This outline illustrates the loading for the big and small skill players during the 2009 calendar year
- The 2009 Season featured the most wins in a single season since Dan Marino was the quarterback in the early 1980s

Winter + Spring

Training Block	A	B		C1	C2	
	Jan	Feb		Mar	Apr	
Practice/Comp	Bowl	None	Break	Spring Ball	Spring Ball	Break
Alactic SPP	Power	Capacity	Break	None	None	Break
Sprints	10-40yd	<=30yd	Break	None	None	Break
Aerobic SPP Big	<=1160wk	variable	Break	AREG	AREG	Break
Aerobic SPP Sm	<=1600wk	variable	Break	AREG	AREG	Break
Aerobic Linear Big	<=1160wk	variable	Break	AREG	AREG	Break
Aerobic Linear Sm	<=1600wk	variable	Break	AREG	AREG	Break
Jumps	Stair Bounds	Box	Break	Box	Box	Break
Explosive Throws						
Press	50-70%	+70%	Break	AREG	AREG	Break
Squat	50-70%	<=70%	Break	AREG	AREG	Break
Auxiliary Weights	High Vol	Med Vol	Break	AREG	AREG	Break
Torso	Up to 800wk	Up to 1000wk	Break	AREG	AREG	Break

Summer + Competition Calendar

Training Block	A1	A2	B	C1	C2	C3	C4	C5
	May	Jun	Jul	Aug	Sep	Oct	Nov	Dec
Practice/Comp	7 on 7	7 on 7	7 on 7	Camp	Comp	Comp	Comp	Comp
Alactic SPP	GPP/Power	Power	Capacity	None	None	None	None	None
Sprints	<=50yd	<=60yd	<=30yd	None	None	None	None	None
Aerobic SPP Big	<=1160wk	1400wk	>700wk	AREG	AREG	AREG	AREG	AREG
Aerobic SPP Sm	<=1600wk	2000wk	>1000wk	AREG	AREG	AREG	AREG	AREG
Aerobic Linear Big	<=1160wk	1400wk	>700wk	AREG	AREG	AREG	AREG	AREG
Aerobic Linear Sm	<=1600wk	2000wk	>1000wk	AREG	AREG	AREG	AREG	AREG
Jumps	3fold SLJ	Hurdle	Box	Box	Box	Box	Box	Box
Explosive Throws	<=40wk							
Press	50-70%	+70%	+70%	AREG	AREG	AREG	AREG	AREG
Squat	50-70%	+70%	<=70%	AREG	AREG	AREG	AREG	AREG
Auxiliary Weights	High Vol	Med Vol	Med Vol	AREG	AREG	AREG	AREG	AREG
Torso	Up to 800wk	1000wk	1000wk	AREG	AREG	AREG	AREG	AREG

2009 Annual Plan for Big and Small Skill Position Players

AREG

1. Signifies the 'auto-regulation' of the training load. Player's 'auto-regulate' the load based upon readiness and training objective consistent with that block

Testing

Test Alactic Capacity via Biodynamic Positional considerations for all Skill Players except Specialists

- Repeat duration, number of repeats per series, recovery interval between repeats, and recovery interval between series must correspond to sport conditions
- [(2-4sec work + 20-40sec rest) x 3-6 repeats] x 5min rest interval between series
- Consider Dynamic Correspondence when constructing test drills:
  - accentuated regions of force production (where in the amplitude/range of motion are the greatest forces produced/incurred)
  - amplitude and direction of movement (range of motion and direction in which resistance must be overcome)
  - dynamics of effort (the nature of the motion specific to the exercise with and without consideration of the forces involved)
  - rate and time of maximum force production (how fast and for how long is the maximum force generated)
  - regime of muscular work (type of muscular activity ergo overcoming, yielding, sustaining, ballistic, etcetera)

<u>**Kick/Punt Test Alactic Power**</u>
- Field goal, punt, and kick off- distance, operation time, and hang time when applicable

Training Block Contents

<u>**Practice and Competition**</u>
- Possibility of Bowl Game and corresponding practices in late December/early January
- Spring Ball practices from mid March to Mid April
- August Training Camp
- Seasonal practices and weekly contests from September to December

<u>**Alactic SPP**</u>

Alactic Power
- 2-4 second working intervals
- Full recoveries between repeats and series
- Develop peak attainable intensity of alactic mechanism via linear and positional movements

Alactic Capacity
- 2-4 second working intervals
- Incomplete recoveries between repeats
- Full recoveries between series
- Develop peak sustainable intensity for repeated bouts of alactic efforts via linear and positional movements

<u>**Sprints**</u>
- Trained via alactic power and capacity regimes in corresponding blocks

<u>**Aerobic SPP**</u>
- Develop oxidative capacity in muscle fibers responsible for mobilizing competitive exercise(s) via positional movements at aerobic intensities beneath the anaerobic threshold
- Active recovery from alactic work
- Improve peripheral vascular network
- Further condition the mechanizing musculo-tendonous-skeletal apparatus for practice and contest demands

<u>**Aerobic Linear**</u>
- Develop oxidative capacity in muscle fibers responsible for mobilizing linear running at aerobic intensities beneath the anaerobic threshold
- Active recovery from alactic work
- Improve peripheral vascular network
- Further condition the mechanizing musculo-tendonous-skeletal apparatus for practice and contest demands

<u>**Jumps**</u>
- Develop explosive and reactive strength in leg/hip extensor muscles
- Utilize jump exercises that incorporate loaded deep knee bend positions which dynamically correspond to sprint acceleration mechanics

<u>**Special Exercises**</u>

Quarterbacks
- Target muscles of the shoulder girdle responsible for mobilizing the throwing action
- Target muscles of the hip girdle responsible for mobilizing the throwing action

Specialists
- Target muscles of the hip girdle responsible for mobilizing the leg swing action

<u>**Primary Weights**</u>

Press
- Horizontal press variations designated as primary strengthener of shoulder girdle
- Method of exercise performance exists as sub-maximal and repeated efforts with strategically programmed

maximal efforts

Squat
- Squat variations designated as primary strengthener of hip girdle and leg extensors
- Method of exercise performance exists primarily as sub-maximal efforts with occasional maximal efforts

<u>Auxiliary Weights</u>
- Target strength and mobility development, maintain suppleness, in muscles that articulate neck, shoulder girdle, upper back, arms, lower back, hip girdle, and legs
- Method of exercise performance ranges from repeated to sub-maximal efforts

<u>Abdominals and Low Intensive Med Ball Throws</u>
- Develop general fitness and muscular endurance about the trunk and hip girdle

INTERNATIONAL RUGBY SEVENS

Between September 2012 and June 2013 I fulfilled a seasonal contract for the Portuguese Rugby Federation. My position was the Senior National Physical Preparation Coach (Preparador Fisico de Seleccao) for the Senior 15's, 7's, and coordinator for the National Academy, Women's National 7's, and Officials.

Subsequent to my arrival in Portugal I was able to secure performance director/programme manager responsibilities with the 15s coach and later with the 7's coach. This responsibility included the following:

- programming and organizational outlines for both physical preparatory as well as technical-tactical trainings
- comprehensive discussions with head coaches and the technical director regarding long term planning strategies and technical-tactical movement foundations
- real time monitoring and management of technical-tactical practices (making live adjustments to various aspects of practice based upon my observation of player movement efficiency)

I made it a point to develop a working proficiency in speaking, reading, and writing Portuguese. As a result, I wrote all training programs in Portuguese (in my elementary version) so I have selected to illustrate only three outlines here as this represents the extent of my willingness to rewrite the tables in English.

Important to note are the range of physical and technical skill sets that any national team coaching staff is faced with when assembling a team of athletes of varying age, playing experience, and even country of residence and language.

Rugby is an amateur sport in Portugal. Thus, all but one player, between the senior 15's and 7's, was either a worker or student (our 15's hooker and team captain was, and still is, an orthopedic surgeon). As a result, an enormous amount of individualization was necessary in order to effectively advance upon the situation. I worked primarily off of outlines, such as the three that are presented here, and subsequently filled in the details on a daily basis relative to the set of circumstances that I was faced with.

While the sport is amateur in Portugal we did possess an advantage in that all of our Portuguese senior national players were permitted by their clubs to train with us at the National Center during the week. This accounted for roughly half of the National Team as many of our forwards were French players who played for professional clubs in France outside of the test matches.

The Portuguese senior players would attend certain practices with their clubs and certain practices with the national team. The national team practices were generally more demanding than their club practices thus I ensured that high/low integrity was maintained as best as possible by seeing to it that their more intensive physical preparatory trainings occurred on the same day as their national team practices.

You will see the actual bullet point summary I provided to the Federation President/Vice President/Technical Director/and Head Coaches. This summary covered the preparation of the 15's and 7's while the subsequent outlines cover the 7's initial Fall training leading into the first tournament; as well as two additional tournaments between late 2012 and early 2013.

PORTUGUESE RUGBY FEDERATION

- The decrease in sprint volumes provides for an increase in skill specific intensity/volume on Mon/Wed/Fri nights
- Tempo volume will gradually rise until final taper

Technical/Tactical Training
- Technical/Tactical Drills must be introduced early in the training; however, not at the expensive of more relevant physically demanding training
- The technical/tactical work may be performed at low physical cost and in this way mechanics are solidified and a large number of repetitions may be performed
- Passing/catching, tackle technique, contact/offload, kicking technique may all be performed at low physical cost by focusing only on body positions and execution
- As the weeks progress, the proportionality between technical/tactical physical demand and speed work physical demand will begin to shift towards prioritizing technical/tactical workloads that include greater physical efforts. The low cost physical technical/tactical outputs that are initially performed will change to higher intensity outputs. As a result, the physical demand of the speed work and multi-directional/agility/evasive ability, in particular, must decrease in order to allow the body to generate, and recover from, the necessary technical/tactical intensities that will be performed closer to the first matches

Linear Speed Development
- Purely Alactic (without lactic acid), full recoveries between each repetition
- 10-30meters
- Primarily conducted on the hill during September in order to set intensity limit (can't sprint as fast up hill)
- Reduced Intensity of hill allows for greater volume per session

Multi-Directional/Agility/Evasive Ability
- Purely Alactic, full recoveries when intensified, smaller recoveries when done during warm up
- < 6seconds of work per repetition
- Conducted on the pitch

Explosive Ability
- Purely Alactic, full recoveries
- Conducted via:
- Explosive Medicine Ball Throws (backward overhead, between legs forward, diving into pole vault pit, rotational)
- Explosive Pushups (up onto plates, down from plates, rebound on and off plates, clapping)
- Explosive Jumps (up stairs, repeated on flat ground, over hurdles)

Combatives/Scrummaging for 15's Forwards
- Striking against bag, double and single arm open palm strikes, alactic, < 6seconds

- Grappler Twists with barbell, alactic, < 6seconds
- Single Man Scrum Device, alactic, <6 seconds

Primary Weight Training

- Basic exercises which require minimal technical demand to allow for greater outputs at lower technical cost
- Presses
- Squats (not for taller players, taller players will leg press or machine squat)
- Leg Press
- Rows/Chins

Auxiliary Weight Training

- Lesser intensity exercises that target muscular development
- Neck
- Traps
- Shoulders/Rotator Cuff
- Arms
- Erectors/Glutes/Hamstrings
- Abdominals/Trunk

Aerobic Running and Multi-Directional Movement Drills

- Tempo runs, conducted at NO FASTER than 75% of top speed for that distance
- Alternate performing pushups or abdominal exercises after each rep followed by walking recovery
- Distances per repetition will vary between 60meters up to 200meters
- Total volume per session will generally not exceed 3200meters

AUSTRALIA TOURNAMENT PREPARATION 2012

Sprints/Jumps/Primary Weights (explosive pushups after primary press, up emphasis weeks 5, 4, down week 3, rebound weeks 2 and 1)

Alactic Agility Drills performed Wednesday in place of linear speed work weeks 4,3,2,1

Week	Monday/Friday Sprints	Jumps	Monday Leg	Bench	PU	SA Row	Trunk	Wednesday Leg	Floor Press	PU	Inv Row	Trunk	Friday Leg	Incline	PU	CS Row	Trunk
5	Hill- 3x10m, 4x20m, 3x30m	Stair Single 2x6-10	2-3x10	60x4x10	4x3	15,12,10	4x	5x5	70x5x5	5x3	5x8	4x	2-3x10	70xRM	5x3	15,12,10	4x
4	Hill- 2x6x20m	Stair Single 4x6-10	2-3x8	65x4x8	4x4	3x12	4x	4x5	65x4x6	4x4	4x10	4x	2-3x8	65xRM	5x4	3x12	4x
3	Hill- 2x5x20m	Stair Bound 4-6x3	2-3x6	70x4x6	4x5	12,10,8	3x	3x5	60x3x8	3x5	3x12	3x	2-3x6	60xRM	5x3	12,10,8	3x
2	Hill/Flat- 2x4x20m	Stair Bound 3-5x3	2-3x6	75x4x5	4x2	3x10	3x	2x5	55x2x10	5x3	2x15	3x	2-3x6	55xRM	5x2	3x10	3x
1	Flat- 6x20m	Stair Bound 2-4x3	2-3x5	80x3x4	3x2	3x8	2x	2x5	50x2x12	4x3	2x15	2x	2-3x5	50xRM	4x2	3x8	2x

Auxiliary Weights/Explosive Med Ball/Tempo

	Week 5 Tuesday	Thursday	Week 4 Tuesday	Thursday	Week 3 Tuesday	Thursday	Week 2 Tuesday	Thursday	Week 1 Tuesday	Thursday
Neck	3x20	3x10	3x15	3x10	3x12	2x10	2x15	2x10	2x12	2x10
Shrug	3x20	3x10	3x15	3x10	3x12	2x10	2x15	2x10	2x12	2x10
Delts/Cuff	3x	3x	3x	3x	3x	2x	2x	2x	2x	2x
Back Raise	3x20	3x10	3x15	3x10	3x12	2x10	2x10	2x10	2x8	2x10
Pull ups	15,12,10	3x12	12,10,8	3x10	10,8,6	2x10	2x12	2x10	2x8	2x10
MB Throws	12	12	10	10	10	10	8	8	8	8
Tempo	4x10x60	4x6x100	3x10x80	4x7x100	4x5x140	3x8x120	4x6x140	4x4x180	2x4x200	5x200

DUBAI TOURNAMENT PREPARATION 2012

High Intensity Trainings

Week	Week of	Speed	Explosive Jumps	Explosive Pushups	Explosive Throws	Monday	Wednesday	Pullups
5	10/22/12	Flying 10 + 10x5-6	Stair Bounds x 3-5x3	Landings x 3-5x3	OHB/BLF/Dive/Rot x 6 each	Squat 3x7 Bench 70% 12,10,8,6	Bench Squat 3x6 Floor Press 3x6	50total
4	10/29/12	Flying 15 + 10x5-6	Stair Bounds x 3-5x4	Landings x 3-5x3	OHB/BLF/Dive/Rot x 5 each	Squat 3x6 Bench 60% 3 x RM	Bench Squat 3x5 Floor Press 3x5	40total<5kg
3	11/05/12	Flying 20 + 10x4-5	Stair Bounds x 3-5x5	Rebounds x 3-5x2	OHB/BLF/Dive/Rot x 5 each	Squat 3x5 Bench 80% 8,6,4,2	Bench Squat 3x4 Floor Press 3x4	30total<10kg
2	11/12/12	Flying 25 + 10x4-5	Stair Bounds x 3-5x6	Rebounds x 3-6x3	OHB/BLF/Dive/Rot x 3 each	Squat 2x5 Bench 70% 2 x RM	Bench Squat 3x3 Floor Press 3x3	20total<15kg
1	11/19/12	Flying 30 + 10x3-5	Stair Bounds x 3-5x7	Rebounds x 3-6x3	OHB/BLF/Dive/Rot x 3 each	Squat 2x4 Bench 90% 4,2,2	Bench Squat 2x3 Floor Press 2x3	20total<20kg
Travel	11/26/12							

Low Intensity Trainings

Week	Week of	Neck	Single Arm Shrug	Chest Supported Row	Shoulders	Grappler	Back Extension	Biceps	Leg Raises	Barbell Rollout
5	10/22/12	10 ea	10 ea	10	10	5 ea	10	10	10	10
4	10/29/12	12 ea	12 ea	12	12	6 ea	12	12	12	12
3	11/05/12	14 ea	14 ea	10	10	7 ea	10	10	10	10
2	11/12/12	16 ea	16 ea	12	12	8 ea	12	12	12	12
1	11/19/12	18 ea	18 ea	10	10	9 ea	10	10	10	10
Travel	11/26/12	20 ea	20 ea	12	12	10 ea	12	12	12	12

Tempo

Week	Week of	Tuesday	Thursday
5	10/22/12	Option 1,2,3, or 4 x 6x100m	Option 1,2,3, or 4x10x60m
4	10/29/12	Option 1,2,3, or 4 x 6x100m	Option 1,2,3, or 4x10x60m
3	11/05/12	Option 1,2,3, or 4 x 6x100m	Option 1,2,3, or 4x10x60m
2	11/12/12	Option 1,2,3, or 4 x 6x100m	Option 1,2,3, or 4x10x60m
1	11/19/12	Option 1,2,3, or 4 x 6x100m	Option 1,2,3, or 4x10x60m
Travel	11/26/12		

NEW ZEALAND TOURNAMENT PREPARATION 2013

Week →	7	6	5	4	3	2	1 Travel
Week of →	17 Dec	24 Dec	31 Dec	7 Jan	14 Jan	21 Jan	28 Jan
Movement ↓	Monday	Monday	Monday	Monday	Monday	Monday	
Tempo	2x6x100m (16-17sec) pushups/abs	3x5x100m (16-17sec) pushups/abs	3x6x100m (16-17sec) pushups/abs	3x7x100m (16-17sec) pushups/abs	4x6x100m (16-17sec) pushups/abs	4x6x100m (16-17sec) pushups/abs	
Tuesday	Tuesday	Tuesday	Tuesday	Tuesday	Tuesday	Tuesday	
Special Endurance	3x(4x60) 90/3min 30m intensity limit	3x(4x60) 90/3min 30m intensity limit	3x(3x60)2min/4min 40m intensity limit	3x(3x60)2min/4min 40m intensity limit	2x(4x60)2.5min/5min 50m intensity limit	2x(4x60)2.5min/5min 50m intensity limit	
Explosive Throws	OHB/BLF/Div x 5	OHB/BLF/Div x 5	OHB/BLF/Div x 4	OHB/BLF/Div x 4	OHB/BLF/Div x 3	OHB/BLF/Div x 3	
Explosive Jumps	Steep Stairs 4x3	Steep Stairs 5x3	Hill Bounds 6x3	Hill Bounds 6x3	Hurdle Hops 6x3	Hurdle Hops 4x3	
Bench Squat	80% bodyweight 5x5	90% bodyweight 4x5	100% bodyweight 3x5	3x4 optional weight	3x3 optional weight	2x3 optional weight	
Bench	60%x5x5	60%+10kgx5x4	60%+20kgx5x3	60%x10x3	60%x8x3	60%x6x3	
Explosive Pushups	Up Only 5x3	Up Only 5x4	Landings 5x5	Landings 10x3	Rebounds 8x3	Rebounds 6x3	
Dumbbell Press	Incline 2x10	Incline 2x15	Floor 2x10	Floor 2x15	Flat 2x10	Flat 2x15	
Rows	15,12,10	3x12	12,10,8	3x10	10,8,6	3x8	
Wednesday	Wednesday	Wednesday	Wednesday	Wednesday	Wednesday	Wednesday	
Tempo	6x100m (16-17sec) pushups/abs	7x100m (16-17sec) pushups/abs	9x100m (16-17sec) pushups/abs	10x100m (16-17sec) pushups/abs	2x6x100m (16-17sec) pushups/abs	2x6x100m (16-17sec) pushups/abs	
Neck	2x10 ea	2x12 ea	2x15 ea	3x10 ea	3x12 ea	3x15 ea	
Trapezius	2x10	2x12	2x15	3x10	3x12	3x15	
Pullups	3x10 bodyweight	4x10 bodyweight	5x10 bodyweight	5x10 5kg	4x10 7.5kg	3x10 10kg	
Back Extension	Double leg 3x10-12	Double Leg 3x12-15	Double Leg 3x15-20	Single Leg 3x10-12	Single Leg 3x12-15	Single Leg 3x15-20	
Shoulders	2x10	2x12	2x15	3x10	3x12	3x15	
Biceps	10,8,6	3x8	12,10,8	3x10	15,12,10	3x12	
Thursday	Thursday	Thursday	Thursday	Thursday	Thursday	Thursday	
Sled Sprint	30mx6, 2min	30mx5, 2.5min	30mx4, 3min	30mx3, 3.5min	30mx3, 3.5min	30mx3, 3.5min	
Explosive Throws	OHB/BLF/Div x 5	OHB/BLF/Div x 5	OHB/BLF/Div x 4	OHB/BLF/Div x 4	OHB/BLF/Div x 3	OHB/BLF/Div x 3	
Explosive Jumps	Steep Stairs 3x3	Steep Stairs 4x3	Hill 4x3	Hill 4x3	Hurdle Hops 4x3	Hurdle Hops 3x3	
Squat	80% bodyweight 3x5	90% bodyweight 3x4	100% bodyweight 3x3	3x4 optional weight	3x3 optional weight	2x3 optional weight	
Bench	60%+10kgx2x2RM	60%+20kgx2xRM	60%+30kgx2xRM	60x5/70x5/80xRM	65x3/75x3/85xRM	70x5/80x3/90xRM	
Explosive Pushups	Up Only 5x2	Up Only 5x2	Landings 5x2	Landings 5x2	Rebounds 5x2	Rebounds 5x2	
Rows	10,12,15	3x10	8,10,12	3x12	6,8,10	3x15	

XIX. SUMMARY

There is no professional coaching endeavor that is capable of superseding the importance of securing biomechanical movement efficiency.

Movement is the commonality shared between all athletes in all sports. Thus the optimization of its efficiency benefits performance advancement as much as the prevention of injury.

Securing biomechanical movement efficiency is only one part of a greater whole; however, which is the omniscient objective of optimizing global training load management.

The coach who seeks to operate at an omniscient capacity assumes a global perspective towards problem solving. This point of view is central towards enhancing the process of deconstructing problems down to the basal level; at which point any possibility for debate is obviated.

Sprinting is one of the basal constituents, arguably the most important, in the preparation of most T&F, team based field and court sport athletes.

Any coach of speed/power athletes is assured to enhance these competition outcomes via the study and practice of applied sprint training.

12 weeks
   4 GPP
   3 MS
   1 Deload
   3 MS
   1 Deload

Target MS
   T-Bar Dead
   RFESS

Target Speed Work
   20-30m or less
   Acceleration or lateral emphasis
   Flux between alactic full rest and alactic 20s rests

Special Endurance
   Slide Board or shuffle

Plyo Progressions
   DL Box /Hill
   SL Box /Drill

   DL Drop
   SL Drop

   DL/SL Drop to Jump

   DL/SL Bounding

Aux. Strength
   Horiz. Push DB /PU
   Pulls

   SL Hip Hinge
   Lateral squat
   Lateral Pronoker

MB Power
   No land ⇒ land